CAMBRIDGE MUSIC

Schumann: *Fantasie*, Op. 17

CAMBRIDGE MUSIC HANDBOOKS

GENERAL EDITOR Julian Rushton

Cambridge Music Handbooks provide accessible introductions to major musical works, written by the most informed commentators in the field.

With the concert-goer, performer and student in mind, the books present essential information on the historical and musical context, the composition, and the performance and reception history of each work, or group of works, as well as critical discussion of the music.

Other published titles

Bach: Mass in B Minor JOHN BUTT
Beethoven: *Missa Solemnis* WILLIAM DRABKIN
Berg: Violin Concerto ANTHONY POPLE
Chopin: The Four Ballades JIM SAMSON
Handel: *Messiah* DONALD BURROWS
Haydn: *The Creation* NICHOLAS TEMPERLEY
Haydn: String Quartets, Op. 50 W. DEAN SUTCLIFFE
Janáček: *Glagolitic Mass* PAUL WINGFIELD
Mahler: Symphony No. 3 PETER FRANKLIN
Musorgsky: *Pictures at an Exhibition* MICHAEL RUSS
Schoenberg: *Pierrot lunaire* JONATHAN DUNSBY
Schubert: *Die schöne Müllerin* SUSAN YOUENS

Schumann: *Fantasie*, Op. 17

Nicholas Marston
Lecturer in Music, Exeter University

Published by the Press Syndicate of the University of Cambridge
The Pitt Building, Trumpington Street, Cambridge CB2 1RP
40 West 20th Street, New York, NY 10011–4211, USA
10 Stamford Road, Oakleigh, Victoria 3166, Australia

First published 1992

Printed in Great Britain at the University Press, Cambridge

A catalogue record for this book is available from the British Library

Library of Congress cataloguing in publication data
Marston, Nicholas.
Schumann: Fantasie, op. 17 / Nicholas Marston.
p.   cm. – (Cambridge music handbooks)
Bibliography
ISBN 0 521 39284 5 (hardback) – ISBN 0 521 39892 4 (paperback)
1. Schumann, Robert, 1810–1856. *Fantasie*, piano, Op. 17, C major.
I. Title. II. Series.
ML410.S4M37 1992
786.2'189–dc20 91–39602 CIP MN

ISBN 0 521 39284 5 hardback
ISBN 0 521 39892 4 paperback

AH

Meinem guten Geist, meinem besseren Ich

Contents

Contents

Plates

Preface

A book on Schumann's *Fantasie*, Op. 17 should require no special pleading. The work's popularity is attested by a distinguished performance history; many of the greatest pianists of the twentieth century have recorded it. It has long been recognized not only as one of Schumann's greatest piano compositions but as one of the central works of the early Romantic period. Yet such fame can result in a weakening of critical attention. In writing this book I have been as surprised by the amount of documentary evidence that has hitherto gone unmentioned or unnoticed as by the generally unadmitted fragility of some of the established 'facts' about the *Fantasie*. On reflection, such surprise is perhaps unmerited. It is only in very recent years that Schumann's music has aroused a level of scholarly interest commensurate with its popularity in performance. Only since the mid 1980s has it been possible to consult a reliable edition of the complete *Tagebücher* and *Haushaltsbücher*, for example; for Schumann's general correspondence one must still rely on Gustav Jansen's edition of 1904, while the new edition of the Robert–Clara *Briefwechsel* remains incomplete at the time of writing. And quite apart from these major *lacunae* in the sources, the quantity and quality of detailed discussions of individual works remains lamentable, particularly for readers confined to literature in English. It is hoped that this book helps to fill the gap.

The main historical discussion is presented in chapters 1 and 7, which thus frame the more specific discussion of the *Fantasie* itself. Chapter 1 deals with the compositional history of the work as this may be reconstructed from correspondence, sketches, and other musical sources; chapter 7 examines the history of the work after its publication. Chapter 1 also provides the seeds for much of the discussion in chapters 2–6: thus, Schumann's constantly changing nomenclature for the work becomes the springboard for the discussion of genre in chapter 2, while his decision to preface the score with a quotation from a poem by Friedrich Schlegel fuels the examination of allusion and quotation in chapter 3. The evidence for an intended cyclical connection

xi

between the first and third movements revealed in the *Stichvorlage* similarly raises the question of inter-movement unity, which is taken up in chapter 5. The central chapter 4 deals at some length with the first movement, which has always attracted the most critical and analytical attention, while chapters 5 and 6 together go some way towards reviving interest in the other two movements, which have on the whole been unfairly neglected.

Since one of my aims has been to raise the level of analytical discussion of the *Fantasie*, I have on occasion found it unavoidable to use terminology and notational devices with which some readers will be unfamiliar. The greatest difficulty is likely to be encountered in connection with examples such as 4.7 (p. 55), which is grounded in the analytical concepts and techniques developed by Heinrich Schenker. Voice-leading (or Schenkerian) analysis holds that the structure of a piece of tonal music, such as the *Fantasie*, is multilayered: that is, the surface, or 'foreground', may be understood as an elaboration of a simpler underlying structure, or 'middleground', which may itself be reduced to simpler structures until an irreducible 'background' structure is revealed. A consequence of this view is that not all events on the surface are regarded equally: some may be of relatively long-range significance while others are regarded as purely local or immediate details helping to 'prolong' the more structural elements. In attempting to express this multilayered conception, analysts bend conventional musical symbols to their own purpose. Unstemmed black noteheads, stemmed black notes (crotchets) and stemmed white notes (minims) denote the structural hierarchy, proceeding upwards from the least to the most important elements; broken slurs (or beams) are used to highlight structural elements – individual notes or complete harmonies – that are operative (while not being constantly present aurally) over a large musical span; *un*broken slurs or beams denote motion from one structural point to another, and the events grouped under a slur can be understood as elements 'prolonging' this larger motion.

As its name implies, voice-leading analysis lays particular emphasis on the *linear*, or contrapuntal, structure of tonal music rather than assuming its structure to be essentially vertical, or harmonic. The musical surface of a work often distorts the underlying linear structure, however: simple 'middleground' contrapuntal progressions may be masked by 'foreground' detail and embellishment; and a particular musical line may begin in one part of the texture and be completed in another. One of the tasks of a voice-leading graph such as Example 4.7 is to help clarify such passages. In order to do this, it is often helpful to represent the notes in the score in simple rearrangements: for example, inner notes within a particular passage may be transferred to a higher octave in order to show that they are part of a line which has begun in the top voice. Readers may find it helpful to play the few examples of voice-leading analysis at the keyboard and to compare their sound closely with that of the relevant passage in the printed score.

Pitch identification

Throughout the text, specific pitches are identified according to the Helmholtz system: C–B, c–b, c¹–b¹, c²–b²... where c¹ = middle C. In chapter 5 certain notes are identified as 'scale degrees' by means of a number combined with a superscript caret. The number identifies the position of the note within the octave scale of the prevailing key: thus C is scale degree $\hat{1}$ in the key of C but scale degree $\hat{5}$ in the key of F.

Formal analyses

Italicized upper and lower-case letters, combined where necessary with numbers or an apostrophe, are used to denote formal sections and subsections: *A*, *A1*, *a*, *a1*, *a'*, etc.

Keys and harmonic functions

Upper-case letters denote major keys; lower-case letters denote minor keys. The expression V/C etc. means V of C, that is, the dominant of C major.

Acknowledgements

I am multiply indebted to Julian Rushton, whose enthusiasm for the *Fantasie* in an undergraduate seminar on the period 1830–50 at Cambridge in 1979–80 first aroused my own serious interest; it is fitting that this book appears under his general editorship. I must also thank, anonymously, the several generations of students who have struggled dutifully to analyse one or other movement of the *Fantasie* at my command, and who have no less dutifully endured my own burgeoning ideas; my colleague Jim Samson endured critically as well as dutifully. Lesley Sharpe, Lecturer in German at Exeter University, kindly read and improved upon my translations from that language. I prepared the music examples using music-processing equipment purchased with a generous grant from the Research Grant Committee at Exeter University. Others who have eased the writing of this book in various ways include the staffs of the British Library Manuscript Students' Room and Photographic Department, Dr Bernhard Appel (Robert-Schumann-Forschungsstelle), Dr Oswald Brill (Hessische Landes- und Hochschulbibliothek, Darmstadt), John Butt, Gerry Bye (Cambridge University Library Photographic Department), Timothy Day (National Sound Archive), Dr Joachim Draheim, Dr Maria Eckhardt (Liszt Memorial Museum and Research Centre, Budapest), Dr Uta Hertin-Loeser (Staatsbibliothek Preussischer Kulturbesitz, Berlin), Birgit Kelber (Universitätsbibliothek, Bonn), Jana Kerkow (Deutsche Staatsbibliothek, Berlin), Dame Moura Lympany, Catherine Massip (Bibliothèque Nationale, Paris), Barbara Mohn, Dr Robert Murányi (National Széchényi Library, Budapest), Dr Gerd Nauhaus (Robert-Schumann-Haus, Zwickau), Stephen Redhead, Dr Stephen Roe (Sotheby's), Dr Linda Correll Roesner, Dr J Rigbie Turner (Pierpont Morgan Library, New York), and Dr Matthias Wendt (Robert-Schumann-Forschungsstelle).

Abbreviations

AMZ	*Allgemeine musikalische Zeitung*
BG	*Briefe und Gedichte aus dem Album Robert und Clara Schumanns*, ed. Wolfgang Boetticher
Bw I, II	Robert and Clara Schumann, *Briefwechsel: kritische Gesamtausgabe*, ed. Eva Weissweiler
D-DS	Darmstadt, Hessische Landes- und Hochschulbibliothek
F-Pn	Paris, Bibliothèque Nationale
GB-Lbl	London, British Library
Grove	*The New Grove Dictionary of Music and Musicians*, ed. Stanley Sadie
GS, I–IV	Robert Schumann, *Gesammelte Schriften über Musik und Musiker*
JNF	*Robert Schumanns Briefe: neue Folge*, ed. F. Gustav Jansen
NZfM	*Neue Zeitschrift für Musik*
SmW	*Signale für die musikalische Welt*
Tb I, II	Robert Schumann, *Tagebücher*
US-NYpm	New York, Pierpont Morgan Library
D-Zsch	Zwickau, Robert-Schumann-Haus

1

The compositional history of the 'Fantasie'

Between 10 and 13 August 1845 the town of Bonn was *en fête*. The reason for the festivities was the unveiling of the Beethoven monument or *Denkmal* on the Münsterplatz. Among those present were Queen Victoria and Prince Albert, and the King and Queen of Prussia. Before the unveiling took place, around midday on 12 August, Beethoven's Mass in C, Op. 86 was sung at a service in the Münsterkirche. At four o'clock there was the second of two concerts directed by Liszt and Spohr, both of whom had played a major role in the monument project. Among the works performed were the 'Emperor' Concerto, conducted by Spohr with Liszt as soloist; the Fifth Symphony; the 'Harp' Quartet; and numerous other pieces, including excerpts from *Christus am Oelberge* and *Fidelio*. One reviewer estimated that the audience numbered some three thousand people, all crammed into a concert hall about two hundred feet in length. Quite apart from the considerable discomfort which the audience must have suffered, they also forfeited the opportunity to witness one of the more visually imposing events of this *Beethoven-Fest*, the illumination of the Rhine at Cologne.[1]

Robert and Clara Schumann planned to attend the celebrations. Schumann's diary records that they left their home in Dresden on 31 July and reached Leipzig that evening. Early the following morning Schumann wrote to Liszt telling him that he would be present in Bonn. But he suddenly became ill, and on 2 August he decided to alter his plans. The trip to Bonn was aborted; while the revels there and in Cologne were continuing, the Schumanns were travelling back to Dresden where they arrived at about 7 o'clock on the evening of 12 August, the very day of the unveiling.[2]

This was not Schumann's only attempt to demonstrate his solidarity with the Beethoven monument project. Indeed, he would have seen a special significance in the unveiling. The monument was not merely a memorial to the composer whom he revered as the fount of the Romantic movement in music; it was also in part the physical realization of the inspiration for his *Fantasie*, Op. 17. The compositional history of the *Fantasie* is closely bound up with the idea of the Beethoven monument, although in the event the work appeared several years before the monument itself. The genesis of the *Fantasie* can be reconstructed from a variety of sources: Schumann's copious correspondence, above all with Clara Wieck; his diaries; the surviving manuscripts of the work; and the first edition, published by Breitkopf & Härtel in 1839. Scrutiny of all these documents allows a detailed picture to emerge; we shall begin with the literary as opposed to the musical sources.

Letters and diary entries

Plans for a monument to Beethoven reach back to 1828, the year after the composer's death, but it was not until 1835 that serious work began.[3] A committee, the *Bonner Verein für Beethovens Monument*, was formed to oversee the project. Members included the influential literary critic August Wilhelm von Schlegel, who was appointed as the first president. (Schlegel's brother Friedrich, himself a major literary theorist of the Romantic school, also features in the history of the *Fantasie*, as will become clear below.) It was under Schlegel's presidency that the committee drew up its first public statement on the project. Dated 'Bonn, on Beethoven's [sixty-fifth] birthday, 17 December 1835', this 'appeal to Beethoven's admirers' (*Aufruf an die Verehrer Beethoven's*) was widely distributed among musicians and others connected with the arts, as well as more generally among influential and wealthy personages. Exactly when Schumann first learned of the project is unclear, but he certainly knew of it by early April 1836, for in that month the front page of his own *Neue Zeitschrift für Musik* was given over to the committee's *Aufruf*.[4]

Not surprisingly, the committee's main task was to raise public funds sufficient to provide for a suitably grandiose monument. The appeal notice solicited private donations and encouraged benefit concerts and stage performances in aid of the cause; in effect, the arts-loving and practising public was exhorted to use any means at its disposal to raise the necessary amount. Nevertheless, the results were disappointing, so much so that in November 1838 a second *Aufruf* was published. The saviour of the project proved to be Liszt, who in November 1839 offered to donate whatever sum remained necessary for the success of the appeal. His contribution of 2,666 Thaler was much the largest single donation: little wonder, then, that he played such a large part in the 1845 celebrations.[5]

Schumann's response to the initial appeal was very enthusiastic. In publishing the *Aufruf* in 1836 he explicitly aligned the *NZfM* with the fundraising effort and provided an editorial address to which donations could be sent.[6] His personal interest in the project went much further. In June 1836 he published the four-part essay *Monument für Beethoven*;[7] and in his diary for 9 September he noted that he had had 'an idea for a contribution for Beethoven'. The 'idea' became a 'Sonata for Beethoven' which Schumann recorded as being 'finished down to the details' by the beginning of December 1836.[8] Later that month, on 19 December, he approached the publisher Carl Friedrich Kistner and wrote as follows about the new composition:

I am addressing myself to you because I know how willing you are to turn your hand to the realization of an attractive idea.

Florestan and Eusebius are keen to do something for Beethoven's monument and for this purpose they have written something under the following title:

Ruins. Trophies. Palms.
Grand Piano Sonata
For Beethoven's Monument
by –

But how is one to contrive that in publishing [the sonata] composer and publisher do not have to pay in cash out of their own pockets, and yet that something remains for the memorial?

Here is what I think. Should you wish to take the work under your wing, I would ask you to send the Bonn committee one hundred complimentary copies, which the committee would soon sell. Let the resulting profit (about 80 Thaler) go towards the monument.

Given the general interest in the affair you would certainly sell enough from your own hand to offset the one hundred presentation copies and the production costs, which should not amount to more than was the case with the earlier sonata [Schumann's Op. 11]. Also, if the production were lavish we could even charge a higher price than normal. It will sell well anyway.

I have my own particular ideas about the design, and given the dignity of the object I think them quite wonderful. A black cover, or better still a binding with a gilt edge, on which these words would stand in gold:

Obolus for Beethoven's Monument

On the main title-page palm leaves could perhaps overhang the principal words. On the following page this would be placed as a dedication:

For B[eethoven]'s Memorial
by

Composer and Publisher

Please – give it some thought: I am on fire about it and can promise that the venture will bring credit to you as well as to me. Moreover, the sonata is noteworthy enough in itself. In the 'Palms' [movement] there is a quotation from the Adagio of the A major symphony. That is all for today, tomorrow I would like to speak with you at greater length about all this. It is my ardent hope that we will soon come to an arrangement and that you will set the matter in hand straight away.[9]

Kistner was evidently unswayed by these grandiose ideas, for by 31 January 1837 Schumann was trying to interest the firm of Tobias Haslinger in the work. On this occasion he committed himself to taking fifty copies while continuing to insist that the monument committee should be given one hundred. Haslinger was no more persuaded than had been Kistner, and on 22 May it was to Breitkopf & Härtel that Schumann turned, though he now made no mention of the Beethoven connection and gave the 'sonata' a new title. He had, he wrote, intended for some time to seek a publisher for two of his compositions: 'One is called "Carnaval"; the other: "Fantasies for Pianoforte".'[10]

All these negotiations are a reminder of the difficulty which Schumann experienced in getting his music accepted for publication at this time. Publishers were wary of its novel, even eccentric features, and exercised a good deal of commercial caution when approached.[11] Nevertheless, Schumann's faith in his new composition remained undiminished. It is next mentioned in a worklist which he entered on the back cover of a diary for the period 28 July 1836 to 28 October 1837.[12] The list consists of a numerical sequence of opus numbers from 1 to 16, the appropriate composition being entered against each number. With the exception of the blank number 6, Opp. 1 to 11 correspond to the works carrying those numbers today. Op. 12, however, is the Sonata in G minor eventually published as Op. 22 in 1839. Opp. 13 and 14 again correspond to their present-day counterparts, while Op. 15 is the 'Sonata for Beethoven' and Op. 16 is a sonata in F minor. Schumann had been sketching a sonata in this key between December 1836 and February 1837; and in March of the latter year he had noted that the Sonata in G minor was in order 'except for the last two pages, which I cannot finish.'[13] The worklist thus represents a catalogue of Schumann's publications and projected publications; and since it does not include the *Davidsbündlertänze* or the *Fantasiestücke*, Op. 12, both of which were composed in the period July–August 1837, it may be that it was written earlier than its position in the diary suggests. Whatever the publishers thought of it, then, Schumann clearly still regarded his 'Sonata for Beethoven' as a viable work in the early months of 1837. In view of its projected numbering as Op. 15 he may even have expected it to appear towards the end of the same year: the *Concert sans orchestre* had appeared as Op. 14 in 1836, and the *Etudes symphoniques* were published as Op. 13 in the middle of 1837.[14]

The 'Sonata for Beethoven' was eventually published as the *Fantasie*, Op. 17. In order to trace the next stages in its compositional history we must examine more closely the publication of the similarly-named *Fantasiestücke*, Op. 12. Schumann recorded in his diary that these pieces had been composed in July 1837. On 6 November he noted that he had 'checked through the Fantasiestücke ready for printing'; and it was presumably some of these same pieces which he had played to a visitor, the cellist Fritz Kummer from Dresden, some days earlier on 1 November.[15] It was not until the following year that Op. 12 actually appeared in print, however: Schumann told Clara on 5 January 1838 that 'the Davids[bündler]tänze and Fantasiestücke will be ready in eight days – I'll send them to you if you want'. The former work was recorded as being ready by 27 January; the latter fared less well, for in a letter of 6–7 February Schumann told Clara, 'I have just received the "Fantasiestücke" from Härtel's', and promised to send them to her on the following Saturday. By the date of her next letter to Schumann, written from Vienna between 2–8 March, Clara had received the *Davidsbündlertänze* and the *Fantasiestücke* and had decided that her favourite pieces from the latter were 'Fabel', 'Aufschwung', 'des Abends', 'Grillen', and 'Ende vom Lied'.[16]

The diary entry covering the period 24–7 January is a particularly happy one: 'hardworking and on excellent form all the time, and lived and composed in raptures over my sweetheart – also looked out the old Fantasiestücke again and tidied them up'.[17] What pieces was Schumann referring to? He could not have meant the *Fantasiestücke*, Op. 12, for these had been 'checked through' back in November 1837 and were now about to appear in print; thus the 'old' pieces must have been the 'Fantasies' offered to Breitkopf & Härtel in May 1837 – in other words, the 'Sonata for Beethoven' of 1836. The title 'Fantasies' reappears in two further letters to Breitkopf & Härtel, written on 4 and 6 February 1838. In the former he told Härtel that 'I am presently occupied very enthusiastically with the completion and partial copying of several new pieces: 2nd piano sonata, – Fantasies for piano, – Novelletten for piano – and 3rd piano sonata, – the only [works] which I propose to publish in the next two years'; in the latter he introduced another potential new title when he referred to 'the Fantasies (which I should like to call *Fata Morgana*)'.[18] Two further sources also capture some of these details. In a laconic diary entry Schumann noted that the *Fantasiestücke*, Op. 12 had appeared in print by 12 February and that he had 'sold my compositions to Breitkopf's'. This is borne out in the *NZfM* for 13 February, which carried a notice from Breitkopf & Härtel announcing that Schumann's '2nd sonata', '2 books of Novelletten', 'Fantasies', and '3rd sonata' were their sole property and were to be published as the composer's Opp. 15–18.[19] Schumann's renewed work on his 'old Fantasiestücke' seems to have occupied him from January to the end of March or thereabouts. On 18 March he wrote to Clara, then in Vienna, recounting his intense compositional activity:

In addition, I have completed a fantasy in three movements which I had sketched down to the last detail in June 1836. The first movement is probably the most passionate thing I have ever written – a deep lament for you – the others are weaker, but need not exactly feel ashamed of themselves. In addition there are Novelletten, three whole books of them – Kinderszenen, which are in fair copy throughout – the Novelletten are likewise ready for printing apart from a few minor details.[20]

There is a complementary entry in the diary for 14–20 March: 'composition must now be put to one side – the Novelletten have still to be put in order – Fantasies and Kinderszenen are in fair copy throughout and will march off to print in a few days'. Finally, in a summary of the period 26–31 March Schumann noted that 'nothing at all out of the ordinary happened during these days – worked hard all the time – checked through the "Dichtungen" '.[21]

Several important issues arise from these last strands of evidence. First there is Schumann's mention of a work called *Dichtungen*, meaning 'poems'. This is yet another intermediate title for the eventual *Fantasie*, Op. 17. The title *Dichtungen* also appears on the title-page of the *Stichvorlage* of the *Fantasie*, from which the first edition was published. Since this copyist's score, which is discussed in more detail below, contains numerous revisions in Schumann's hand, it must have been precisely this manuscript which he had been checking through at the end of March. This is also suggested by a letter to Clara which occupied Schumann between 14 April and 9 May 1838. In a section written on Easter Monday, 16 April, he wrote: 'Then the next thing to appear in print are Fantasies, which I have called "Ruins, Triumphal Arch and Constellation" and "Poems", however, so as to distinguish them from the Fantasiestücke [Op. 12]. I searched for that last word [*Dichtungen*] for a long time before finding it; I think it a very noble and significant term for musical compositions.'[22] From this it emerges that beyond giving the work a new general title Schumann had renamed the second and third movements, formerly called 'Trophies' and 'Palms'.

Secondly, there are various discrepancies between Schumann's letter of 18

March 1838 and his diary entries for 1836. In the letter he claimed that the 'fantasy' had been written in June 1836; but the diary entries quoted above record that his 'idea for a contribution for Beethoven' occurred on 9 September 1836, and that he had finished the 'Sonata for Beethoven' at the beginning of December. Obviously, by early 1838 Schumann may simply have forgotten the exact date of composition back in 1836; but this seems unlikely in view of his extraordinarily careful diary-keeping throughout most of his life. Thus we should perhaps reconsider the 'idea . . . for Beethoven' of September 1836. The remark need not necessarily record Schumann's very first idea for the work which became the *Fantasie*. He may already have begun composing it in the summer of 1836 and only subsequently have conceived the way in which it might serve to raise money for the Beethoven monument project. Allied to the apparent discrepancy in dating is the mismatch between what Schumann told Clara of his inspiration for the work, or at least its first movement – 'a deep lament for you' – and what he told his diary and Kistner: the work was a 'sonata for Beethoven'. The letter to Clara of 18 March 1838 makes no mention of the Beethoven connection whatsoever. Was Schumann silently rewriting events now that the intended fund-raising object of the work was no longer relevant? In effect, was the original inspiration for the *Fantasie* Beethoven or Clara? One might point initially to the strong musical reasons, centring on the celebrated allusion to the final song of Beethoven's *An die ferne Geliebte* in the first movement of the *Fantasie*, for believing that this movement is indeed a response to Schumann's enforced separation from Clara in 1836.[23] But the true explanation is probably rather less straightforward.

A crucial piece of evidence is provided by Schumann's autograph score of the first movement. This manuscript is inaccessible at present, but descriptions of it are available.[24] According to these the title-page originally read *Ruines. Fantaisie pour le Pianoforte dediée à* [obliterated name] *par Robert Schumann Op. 16a*. This ink title was crossed out in red crayon and the following substituted in that medium: *Ruinen, Trophaeen, Palmen. Grosse Sonate für das Pianoforte für Beethovens Monument von Florestan u.[nd] Eusebius Op. 12*. This revised title is almost identical with the one Schumann gave Kistner in his letter of 19 December 1836. The most important point, though, is that comparison of the two titles strongly suggests that Schumann originally composed the first movement as an independent 'fantasy' called *Ruines*. The addition of two further movements and German titles for all three came only later. Moreover, in June 1836 Schumann had very good reason to compose a passionate piece of music with this title. In that month he and Clara, acting on Wieck's orders, returned their love letters to one another. Wieck was even scheming, with some success, to make Schumann believe that Clara no longer cared for him. A further blow to Schumann must have been Clara's failure, again owing entirely to paternal pressure, to respond to the presentation copy of his Sonata in F♯ minor, dedicated 'to Clara from Florestan and Eusebius', which he had sent her in June. His distress is made abundantly clear in a letter written to his friend Anton von Zuccalmaglio on 2 July, in which he apologizes for having been out of contact for so long and blames his silence on the 'deep emotional pain' which he has been suffering and out of which he has been unable to lift himself in order to work: 'at last music, my own inward creative [musical] urge . . . brought me strength and courage again'. His life must have seemed to him to be quite literally in ruins.[25]

Although the autograph manuscript of the first movement of the *Fantasie* is undated, then, we may confidently surmise the following series of events. In June 1836 Schumann composed a 'deep lament' for Clara which he called 'Ruins' and intended to publish as Op. 16a. Subsequently, in September, he had the idea of using this composition as part of a work to raise funds for the Beethoven monument. He wrote two further movements, and the 'Sonata for Beethoven' with movements called *Ruinen*, *Trophaeen*, and *Palmen* was ready to be offered to Kistner by the beginning of December. Thus it was Clara who inspired the first movement and Beethoven who inspired the other two. And the continuing autobiographical significance of that first movement is surely shown by the fact that it uniquely retained its title in 1838 when Schumann altered those of the last two movements to 'Triumphal Arch' (*Siegesbogen*) and 'Constellation' (*Sternbild*) and renamed the entire work 'Poems' (*Dichtungen*). His remark to Clara on 18 March 1838 that he has 'completed a fantasy in three movements which I had sketched down to the last detail in June 1836' is not strictly true, therefore; yet it hides an important truth about the genesis of the *Fantasie* which seems hitherto to have gone quite unsuspected.

After revising the *Stichvorlage* of *Dichtungen* towards the end of March 1838, Schumann must have sent it off to Breitkopf & Härtel. On 6 July he wrote to Raimund Härtel asking him to send back the manuscript of *Dichtungen* because he wished to change the title.[26] Precise details of the change were not forwarded until 19 December, however, when Schumann, now in Vienna, again wrote to Breitkopf & Härtel to inform them that the work was to be published as 'Fantasy . . . Op. 17'.[27] Schumann's eagerness to see the work in print is evident in his next letter, dated 6 January 1839, in which he reminded Breitkopf & Härtel that they had numerous works of his in their hands: 'If it is at all possible for you, please commit yourselves truly to speedy publication of the Fantasy dedicated to Liszt, following which you might then like to put out the Novelletten after a little while.'[28] And to Clara he wrote on 26 January that 'the Kinderszenen have now appeared; also soon to appear is the Fantasy (of which you know nothing) which I wrote during our unhappy separation and which [is] excessively melancholy; it is dedicated to Liszt'. Clara was eager to see the new work, for on 28 February she wrote to Schumann asking whether he might wish to use some passing opportunity to send her a copy of it and of his other new compositions.[29]

Breitkopf & Härtel were ready to meet Schumann's demands, for on 2 March Schumann wrote to Härtel informing him that he had that day sent off the corrected proofs of the 'Fantasy' by fast mailcoach. On 13 March he promised Clara that he would send it and the other pieces by post from Leipzig, if this would not be too expensive for her.[30] 'Publication of Kinderszenen and proofreading of the Fantasiestücke' is mentioned in the diary for 20 March, on which day Schumann again wrote to the publishers, this time concerning arrangements for posting copies of the 'Fantasy' once it was published. If these could be in his hands in Vienna by 4 April, he would forward one to Liszt in Rome. If not, he requested that no copies be sent to Vienna, for he was leaving there on 5 April and would not be returning to Leipzig until the middle of the month.[31] On his way back to Leipzig, he reported to Clara on 7 April that 'the Fantasy is already [finished] at Härtel's; I will send it to you immediately from Leipzig, together with the paper [the *NZfM*] and perhaps my picture, that is, if you want it'; and a further letter, written from Leipzig on 10 April, states that he had arrived there early the previous day.[32] By 17 April he had changed the arrangement: Mendelssohn was now to take the 'Fantasy' and the paper as far as Frankfurt (Clara was in Paris at this time). Schumann remarked: 'You can understand the Fantasy only if you think back to the unhappy summer of 1836, when I renounced you; now I have no reason to compose such unhappy and melancholy music.' From a subsequent letter it appears that Mendelssohn left Leipzig on 23 April, and Schumann estimated that the 'Fantasy' would be with Clara by the end of the month.[33] However, it was not until 22 May that Clara first saw the score, as she wrote to Schumann on the following day:

Yesterday I received your wonderful Fantasy – today I am still half ill with rapture; as I played through it I was drawn involuntarily towards the window, and there I felt like leaping out to the beautiful spring flowers and embracing them. I dreamed a beautiful dream during your Fantasy. The March is enchanting, and bars 8–16 on page 15 [that is, bars 8–16 of the second movement] make me quite beside myself; just tell me what you were thinking of in them? I have never had such a feeling, I heard a full orchestra, I can't tell you how I felt. It hurt me much and made me unhappy to think how long it is since I heard a single note of yours – and yet your notes are still so vivid in my memory! Don't you want to arrange the March for orchestra?[34]

More prosaically, Breitkopf & Härtel announced in the *NZfM* for 17 May 1839 that the 'Fantasy for Piano by Robert Schumann Op. 17' had 'just appeared'.[35]

Clara lost no time in getting to work on the new piece. By 28 May she could tell Schumann: 'I have already learned the March from the Fantasy and revel in it! If only I could hear it played by a large orchestra! I'm always going hot and then cold again in it. Do tell me what kind of inspiration is in you.' And on 4 June she once again enthused about the work, and especially the second movement: 'I always play the Fantasy with true rapture, with such truly inner delight – the March, Robert, is really sublime.'[36] Schumann, on the other hand, was more interested in Clara's response to the first movement: understandably so, in view of the events which had inspired it. Replying to her on 9 June he asked: 'Write and tell me what you think to yourself in the *first* movement of the Fantasy. Does it also conjure up many pictures for you? I like the melody [bars 65–7 are notated] best of all. Are not *you* really the 'note' in the motto? I almost believe you are.'[37] The 'motto' in question was a quotation from a poem by Friedrich Schlegel with which Schumann had prefaced the score; Clara's earlier comments about Schumann's 'notes' [*Töne*] are also to be understood as punning references to Schlegel's text:

Durch alle Töne tönet	Through all the notes
Im bunten Erdentraum	In earth's many-coloured dream
Ein leiser Ton gezogen	There sounds one soft long-drawn note
Für den, der heimlich lauschet.[38]	For the one who listens in secret.

This may serve as a bridge from the literary to the musical sources for the *Fantasie*, for the latter show that the motto was not part of Schumann's original conception of the work.

The sketches

Study of Schumann's sketches is still in its infancy. It is important to establish over the Schumann sketch sources the bibliographical control achieved in relation to Beethoven's sketches in recent years. All the sources must be located, identified and 'reconstructed': that is, their original physical state when used by Schumann must be discovered. Only then will it be possible to begin to understand the relationship of the sketches to the finished works.

Example 1.1: Berlin, Deutsche Staatsbibliothek,
Mus. ms. autogr. Schumann 35, 4 [verso]

Example 1.2: Berlin, Deutsche Staatsbibliothek,
Mus. ms. autogr. Schumann 35, 4

(a) [recto], st. 7/8: sketch for an Allegro in E♭

(b) [verso], st. 1: sketch for a Scherzo (cf. Example 1.1)

(c) [verso], st. 3: draft for the *Im Legendenton* (cf. Example 1.1)

All that can be offered here is a brief account of the known sketches for the *Fantasie* together with some representative transcriptions.[39]

The Deutsche Staatsbibliothek in Berlin holds two miscellaneous collections of Schumann sketch manuscripts, known today as Mus. ms. autogr. Schumann 35 and 36. The fourth item in ms. 35 is a single leaf of ten-stave paper. On one side there are two sketches in E♭ major. The first is headed 'Quasi Rondo zur C-Dur Sonate' and the second, which is much longer, is labelled simply *All[egr]o* followed by an illegible word. The other side of the leaf is transcribed complete in Example 1.1. Here the first six bars, all deleted, record part of a Scherzo in F major. The remainder of the material relates closely to the *Im Legendenton* from the first movement of the *Fantasie*. The first five bars correspond to bars 216–20, and the remainder, beginning on staves 3 and 4, consists of a draft corresponding closely to bars 174–207. It is difficult to believe that the draft did not continue on one or more leaves which perhaps no longer survive.

To assess this material accurately it would be necessary to know whether all

Example 1.3: Bonn, Universitätsbibliothek, Schumann 14
[Wiede Sketchbook II], folio 10r

darin selig geschwärmt, als ich krank war
Trio zur Polonaise
?
[two illegible words]

the sketches on the leaf were made contemporaneously, and to date them. Assuming that they were written as a group, the mention of a sonata in C and the appearance of movements in E♭ seem significant in relation to the *Fantasie*, where these keys are used for the three movements. Moreover, C minor, the key of the *Im Legendenton*, is the relative minor of E♭ major as well as being the parallel minor to the tonic key of the entire work. Another striking feature is the apparent use of a motivic link between several of the projected movements on the leaf. The four-note semiquaver figure found in the *Im Legendenton* draft (it also occurs in the final version) uses a lower neighbour-note motion which also characterizes four-note groups in the Scherzo and Allegro sketches (Example 1.2).

Among the best-known Schumann sketch sources are the so-called Wiede sketchbooks, now owned by the Universitätsbibliothek in Bonn. Recent research has argued that only books IV and V are sketchbooks in the sense that they were bound as books when Schumann used them; the others consist for the most part of relatively random assemblages of leaves which had been used before being collected together, and the term 'sketchbook' has been described as 'totally inapplicable' to book II.[40] It is on folio 10r of this source, however, that a further sketch for the *Fantasie* is to be found (Example 1.3).[41]

After the first bar, the material relates very closely to bars 34–35 of the third movement of the *Fantasie*, although the time signature is 3/4 rather than 12/8 and the right-hand melody lacks the exact rhythmic and melodic profile of the final version. The sketch is dated 30 November [18]36, and Schumann noted that he had 'wallowed blissfully in it while I was ill'.[42] The dating is suspicious, since Schumann's diary holds that the 'Sonata for Beethoven' was completed down to the last detail by the beginning of December 1836. Even bearing in mind Schumann's remarkable compositional facility when he was inspired, it seems surprising that something so basic as the time signature of the third movement was not fixed by the end of November. More curious still is the labelling of the sketch as a Trio for a Polonaise. One possible explanation for these anomalies is that Example 1.3 was not actually written as a sketch for the *Fantasie*: it was simply an idea which Schumann noted down, probably after improvising at the piano, and returned to some time later when he was writing the third movement of the *Fantasie*. Thus the date attached to the sketch would reflect not its original notation but the day on which Schumann adopted it for a different compositional purpose.

Only two further sketch sources for the *Fantasie* are presently known. The Wiede Collection apparently still preserves early sketches.[43] And a twelve-stave leaf auctioned in Germany in November 1930 and presently untraced clearly belongs to the phase at which Schumann was trying to interest Kistner in his 'Sonata for Beethoven'. The leaf apparently has six bars of music in C major and 3/4 time headed *Fantasie Andante*, and five bars in 2/2 time and F minor. Whether or not the C major material relates to the *Fantasie*, Op. 17 or to some other projected .work cannot be ascertained. Aside from these musical ideas, however, the leaf also bears the words *Obolen auf Beethovens Monument. Ruinen. Tropheen. Palmen.* Grosse Sonate für das Pianoforte. *Für Beethovens' Monument von Florestan u.[nd] Eusebius. Op. 12* and a note which reads '100 copies for the committee'.[44] The relationship of these verbal entries to Schumann's letter to Kistner is obvious (see above, p. 3). Indeed, this leaf may have formed the title-page of the 'Sonata for Beethoven' as it existed in Schumann's manuscript at that time. If so, we may be confident that on turning the title-page Kistner's eyes would have fallen on the first page of the next manuscript to be discussed.

The autograph manuscript of the first movement

This manuscript was auctioned at Sotheby's in London on 23 November 1977 (lot 191), and again precisely seven years later in a sale held on 22–3 November 1984 (lot 534). It is presently (1991) in an anonymous private collection. Its inaccessibility to scholars is regrettable: Schumann's letters and diaries alone reveal how complex the genesis of the *Fantasie* was, and this manuscript could certainly shed much light on the composition of the first movement. In essence, the two Sotheby's catalogue entries contain all the information about the manuscript that is in the public domain. Fortunately a different page of the manuscript was published to illustrate each catalogue, so that a limited first-hand examination of its contents is possible. The two photographs are reproduced as Plates 1 and 2.

The 1977 entry states that the manuscript consists of '10½ pages including title', and mentions that 'the fold of the first sheet [is] split'; the 1984 entry, on the other hand, gives the total as twelve pages, mentions a 'front cover' which is also referred to as the 'title-page', and records that the 'front and back pages [are] detached'. Combining these details, we may cautiously surmise that the manuscript is made up from six bifolia (double leaves) collected into a single gathering, the outer bifolium (pages 1/2 and 11/12) having since become split down its central fold. Page 1 serves as the title-page or 'front cover', and the music presumably begins on page 2, finishing half way down page 12: ten and a half pages of music, leaving half of the final page for an 'autograph sketch of eight bars in red crayon on verso of the last leaf', as the 1977 entry puts it; the 1984 entry suggests that this sketch is 'probably for another piece or movement'. There are ten staves per page, ruled into five systems in each case. The main text is written in black ink, with red crayon (or pencil) being used in addition to ink for the numerous revisions throughout. As well as being written on the score itself (and sometimes extending into the margins), some revisions are written on paste-overs: four bars on page 5, two and a half extra bars added on page 7. The final four bars have been revised and extended to ten bars.

The details of the title were discussed above but may be repeated here. Schumann first wrote, in ink, *Ruines. Fantaisie pour le Pianoforte dediée à* [deleted name] *par Robert Schumann Op. 16a*. This clearly relates to the first movement of the *Fantasie* only, and implies that the manuscript dates from June 1836, when Schumann composed that movement in the depths of his despair over Clara. At that stage he envisaged the *Fantaisie* as a single-movement work, but later in 1836 he added the second and third movements. The revised title-page inscription dates from this stage: written in red crayon, with which the earlier French inscription has been deleted, it reads *Ruinen, Trophäen, Palmen[.] Grosse Sonate für das Pianoforte Für Beethovens Monument von Florestan u.[nd] Eusebius Op. 12*. This version accords closely with the title which Schumann proposed to Kistner on 19 December 1836. Certain of these details are repeated on the first page of music, as can be seen from Plate 1. The title *Ruinen* (or *Ruines?*) is deleted, as are the inscriptions *Robert Schumann Op. 16* and (above these) *Florestan und Eusebius Op. 12*.[45] Above the latter inscription, finally, is written *Robert Schumann Op. 15*, and this is *not* deleted. The opus number 15, although absent from the title-page of the manuscript, corresponds to the number which Schumann gave to the 'Sonata for Beethoven' in the worklist in his diary for July–October 1837. The preparation of that list and the matching opus number in the autograph manuscript are presumably contemporaneous; the opus number 15 may be connected with Schumann's offer of the work to Breitkopf & Härtel on 22 May 1837.

An intriguing question posed by the title-page of this manuscript concerns the identity of the dedicatee, whose name has been obliterated. Although this matter cannot properly be discussed until the manuscript again becomes available for study, some speculation is possible. Schumann included no dedication in the title which he gave to Kistner. Or rather, the title 'Grosse Sonate . . . für Beethovens Denkmal' itself contains the dedication: Beethoven was surely the intended dedicatee at this stage. This is significant, for it suggests that the obliterated dedication in the manuscript belongs to the period June 1836 and not later. Now when the *Fantasie* was eventually published it bore a dedication to Liszt. This might seem appropriate in view of Liszt's close involvement in the later stages of the Beethoven monument appeal; but Liszt was not party to the initial workings of the appeal committee, and it seems anyway that the dedication of the *Fantasie* to him was prompted more by his favourable opinion of Schumann's music and his dedication to Clara of his own 'Paganini' Etudes, events which belong to the years 1837–8.[46] The obvious dedicatee in June 1836 would naturally have been Clara herself.

If Plates 1 and 2 are typical, the manuscript would appear to be neatly written and eminently legible except where revisions are involved. Despite its overall tidiness, Schumann felt it necessary to have a copy made for the purpose of engraving. Plates 1 and 2 contain several instructions for the copyist. Over the very first system of music Schumann wrote 'I request the copyist to write out *only the notes*'. This is characteristic: Schumann preferred to enter tempi, accents, dynamic markings and so on by himself, a preference which indicates the emphasis he placed on such details. And along the bottom margin of Plate 1 he drew attention to the first major revision in the score (at bars 13–14) and informed the copyist that such crossed-out passages were to be left blank in the copy. A further note was necessitated by his indecision over bars 154–6. As far as can be deduced from Plate 2, these were originally written as they stand in the final version. Schumann later decided to cut from the fifth semiquaver in bar 154 directly to the last three semiquavers in bar 156, so he crossed out the unwanted passage in red pencil. Subsequently he decided that the deleted passage was to be reinstated, so next to it in the margin he directed that the 'red [passage] is to be copied out'.[47]

When Plates 1 and 2 are compared with the published score, the textual variants which leap to the eye make one all the more impatient to study the autograph manuscript in full. Schumann's original tempo heading was simply *Allegretto*, but for this he substituted *Mit durchaus heftiger Empfindung und ganz frei vorzutragen* ('to be performed with the most intense feeling and entirely freely'); the published version reads *Durchaus phantastisch und leidenschaftlich vorzutragen* ('to be played imaginatively and passionately throughout'), with the word *phantastisch* carrying the same overtones of improvisatory freedom as expressed by the earlier *ganz frei* marking. Moreover, Plate 2 shows that in June 1836 Schumann called the central section of the movement *Romanza* rather than *Im Legendenton*. There are significant differences of dynamic marking: note the *piano* left-hand opening and the *poco a poco crescendo* beginning in bar 3, for example, or the markings *mit innigster Empfindung* ('with the most intense feeling') and *Ardamente sempre* at bars 10 and 19 respectively. There are also changes to the notes themselves; but these are better considered in relation to the copy made from this manuscript.

The *Stichvorlage*

A *Stichvorlage* is the text of a musical composition – whether in the composer's hand or that of a copyist – from which the first edition was engraved. In the early part of his career Schumann was often unable to afford the services of a copyist, with the result that his autograph manuscript had to serve as the *Stichvorlage*. In the case of the *Fantasie* he did have a professional copy prepared; and unlike the autograph manuscript of the first movement, this *Stichvorlage* for the entire work is available to scholars.

The *Stichvorlage* for the *Fantasie* is in the National Széchényi Library in Budapest, where it is catalogued as Ms. Mus. 37.[48] With one exception, all the paper is fairly heavy and has a pronounced blue-green colour; there are ten staves (grouped as 5 × 2) per page, and no watermark is visible. The exception is formed by a strip of paper pasted along the bottom margin of folio 15r. This is lighter in colour and weight, and has a slightly narrower stave ruling. The music is written out on a series of seven ungathered bifolia which are foliated 2–15. Folio 1 consists of a single leaf of paper. Although it contains no music, each system is provided with a simple left-hand brace, presumably in Schumann's hand (the copyist's braces in the rest of the manuscript are more elaborate): this may have been a discarded leaf from another manuscript which Schumann used as the title-page of this *Stichvorlage*. On the recto he wrote:

Dichtungen
Für das Pianoforte

— . —

H[er]rn. Franz Liszt
zugeeignet
von
Robert Schumann.
Op. 16

But the opus number has been changed to 17 and *Dichtungen* replaced by *Fantasie*. These changes were made by Breitkopf & Härtel in late December 1838, for on 19 December Schumann had told them: *'Fantasy* for Pianoforte would be a better name for the composition entitled "Dichtungen". The dedication reads to Liszt. The opus number of the Fantasy is Op. 17.[49] On the verso of the title-page Schumann copied out the 'motto', the closing quatrain from Schlegel's *Die Gebüsche*, and in a bracketed note he directed that this should likewise be placed on the verso of the title-page in the printed edition. In fact it was placed at the head of the first movement and given the label 'motto', which does not appear here in the *Stichvorlage*.

Folios 2–15 reveal evidence of three hands, that of the copyist naturally being predominant. Following Schumann's instructions in his autograph manuscript, the copyist confined himself to copying out the notes, which he did beautifully in black ink. He also followed Schumann's wishes in leaving blank those parts of the autograph score which had been deleted. Thus, the first two beats of the left hand in bar 14 of the first movement and all of the right hand were added by Schumann. As Plate 1 shows, it was precisely here that the first major deletion had occurred in the autograph manuscript, causing Schumann to add his instruction to the copyist. As well as completing the musical text in this way, Schumann went through the *Stichvorlage* adding expression marks, phrasing, dynamics and so on. Most of these markings are in ink also, but some, notably pedalling indications, are written in pencil. The third hand found in the score is that of the engraver, who pencilled in page breaks and other details of the layout for the printed edition.

Easily the most fascinating part of the *Stichvorlage* occurs on folio 15. To begin with, the copyist accidentally left out a whole system in the manuscript from which he was copying: it was this system, containing bars 120–4, which Schumann supplied in his own hand on the strip of manuscript paper pasted in along the bottom of folio 15r. Starting with the final bar on this folio, there are signs of a major revision. The final bar corresponds to bar 138 of the third movement, but the second half is different and there follows a double bar and

Example 1.4a: first movement, bars 303–7

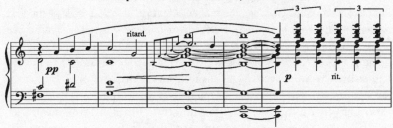

Example 1.4b: third movement, bars 147–51
as originally copied in the *Stichvorlage*

Example 1.4c: *Stichvorlage*, verso of collette on folio 15r

a change of time signature to C (4/4). This heralds a repeat of the last fifteen
bars (295–309) of the first movement, beginning on folio 15v.[50] The repeat is
not quite literal, though, the most telling alteration being the rewriting of bars
300–1 and 303–4 whereby the falling fourth, c^2–g^1, in the melody is replaced
by a fifth, c^2–f^1. The necessary reharmonization produces a slightly different
left-hand part in the following bars, with the seventh G–f replacing the octave
G–g found in bars 305–7 of the first movement. Conversely, while the right-
hand chords in bar 307 of the first movement span the ninth f^2–g^3, the span
is restricted to the octave g^2–g^3 in the version copied in the *Stichvorlage* at the

end of the third movement (compare Examples 1.4a and 1.4b, from which the final two bars of the *Stichvorlage* version, identical to bars 308–9 of the first movement, have been omitted). Such tiny details alert us to the significance of the music on the verso of the strip, or 'collette', at the bottom of folio 15r (Example 1.4c). These four bars in Schumann's hand correspond to the last four written by the copyist: the left hand again has the seventh G–f, although the right retains the ninth span of the first-movement chords. This strip of paper must have come from the autograph score of the third movement: after receiving the *Stichvorlage* Schumann would have checked it against the autograph and noticed the copyist's omission of bars 120–4. Having decided to rewrite the ending of the movement, he cut out the strip containing the last four bars from his own score (and accidentally excised the top notes of the chords in bar 151, which have been supplied editorially in Example 1.4c) and used the blank reverse side to supply the omitted bars. Then he deleted the existing ending in the *Stichvorlage* and wrote out the definitive one (bars 138–42 in the printed score) after it.

This suppressed ending for the third movement is not the only significant change revealed by the *Stichvorlage*. It also provides further evidence of Schumann's changing ideas about the titles of the movements and their particular characters. Schumann's description of the three movements as 'Ruins, Triumphal Arch and Constellation' in his April 1838 letter to Clara is reflected here: the titles *Ruinen, Siegesbogen* and *Sternbild* were entered by the copyist in the centre at the head of each movement only to be deleted by Schumann, who in the bottom margin of folio 2r instructed the engraver to replace each title with a triangular device of three stars.[51] In addition to suppressing the movement-titles, Schumann also revised the tempo indications. The first movement is headed *Durchaus phantastisch und leidenschaftlich vorzutragen*, as in the first edition; there is no sign of either of the two headings found in the autograph manuscript (see above). Both the second and third movements preserve earlier headings: in the former, *Rührig und glänzend* ('brisk and brilliant') was replaced by *Mässig. Durchaus Energisch* ('*Moderato*. Energetic throughout') and in the latter *Einfach und getragen* ('simple and solemn') gave way to *Langsam Getragen[.] Durchweg leise zu halten* ('Slow and solemn. To be kept soft throughout').[52]

While Schumann suppressed the individual movement titles, he continued to experiment with names for the central section of the first movement, which he had called *Romanza* in the autograph score. This term does not occur in the *Stichvorlage*, however. The copyist first wrote *Legende* ('Legend'). Schumann deleted this in pencil and replaced it with *Erzählend im Legendenton* ('narrating in the manner of a legend'). Subsequently he deleted *Erzählend*, changed the initial letter of *im* from lower to upper case, and also made the T of '*-ton*' upper case (and thus a separate word) to give *Im Legenden Ton*.[53]

Conclusion

Schumann composed the first movement of the *Fantasie*, calling it *Ruines. Fantaisie* . . . in June 1836 while in the depths of despair about his enforced separation from Clara. The other two movements were probably composed in the autumn and were inspired by Schumann's plan to compose a work to raise money for the Beethoven Monument Appeal. The entire work was finished by the beginning of December 1836, and later that month Schumann tried to interest Kistner in publishing it as a 'Sonata for Beethoven'. This proposal foundered, and during 1837 overtures were made to Haslinger and then Breitkopf & Härtel, who agreed to publish it. Schumann 'looked out the old Fantasiestücke again and tidied them up' between 24–7 January 1838; on 18 March he told Clara that he had completed a Fantasy which dated from June 1836. At this stage the three-movement work was called *Dichtungen*; Schumann sent the *Stichvorlage* to Breitkopf & Härtel in late March or early April, although further changes (notably to the title) were made later in the year. Proofreading of the first edition was done in February and March 1839, and the *Fantasie*, Op. 17 appeared either at the end of March or in early April.

All that remains to be considered is the exact relationship of the *Stichvorlage* to the autograph manuscript, of which only the first movement is now known. The *Stichvorlage* was probably prepared in 1838 rather than in 1836, at which time Schumann presumably intended his autograph manuscript to serve as *Stichvorlage*. Thus the revisions to the autograph of the first movement were made with the preparation of the *Stichvorlage* in mind. The diary reference to 'Fantasies' being 'in fair copy throughout' must refer to the *Stichvorlage*, which Schumann was apparently then (*c.* 20 March) ready to send off to Breitkopf & Härtel after having made the necessary additions and revisions. An important part of his preparations for the dispatch of the *Stichvorlage* must have been the preparation of the new title-page, complete with its title *Dichtungen* and the Schlegel motto on the verso.

There is a shred of evidence to suggest when Schumann might have come across the motto. Each issue of the *NZfM* carried a quotation, often from a poem or other literary text, on its front page beneath the title. The issue for 27 February 1838 – a period in which Schumann must have been occupied with revising *Dichtungen* – carried the first verse of Schlegel's poem *Bündnis*

('Pact'), with the first line slightly rewritten.[54] Two editions of Schlegel's poems would have been available to Schumann. Whichever he chose, he would have found *Die Gebüsche* from *Abendröte*, from which he took the motto for *Dichtungen*, some twenty pages before *Bündnis*. The evidence cannot be conclusive; but the quotation from *Bündnis* shows that Schumann had more than one reason to be browsing through Friedrich Schlegel's poetry early in 1838.

'What's in a name?' Genre and title in the 'Fantasie'

One of the most conspicuous elements in the compositional history of the *Fantasie* is Schumann's changing nomenclature for the work. The catalogue of names runs as follows:

1) In June 1836 Schumann wrote a one-movement *Fantaisie* entitled 'Ruins' (*Ruines*).

2) By December he had added two movements and offered the entire work to Kistner as a 'Sonata for Beethoven'. The individual movements were called 'Ruins' (*Ruinen*), 'Trophies' (*Trophäen*), and 'Palms' (*Palmen*), and the whole work was described as an 'Obolus for Beethoven's Monument'.

3) In May 1837 he offered it to Breitkopf & Härtel, as 'Fantasies' (*Phantasieen*).

4) In January 1838 he referred in his diary to 'the old Fantasiestücke' (*die alte Phantasiestücke*).

5) Writing to Breitkopf & Härtel on 6 February he mentioned the 'Fantasies' (*Phantasieen*), which he now wished to call *Fata Morgana*.

6) Writing to Clara on 18 March he referred to 'a Fantasy (*Phantasie*) in three movements'.

7) On 16 April he told Clara that he now intended to call the 'Fantasies' (*Phantasien*) by the names 'Ruins' (*Ruinen*), 'Triumphal Arch' (*Siegesbogen*), and 'Constellation' (*Sternbild*), and that the whole work was to be called 'Poems' (*Dichtungen*) in order to distinguish it from the already published *Fantasiestücke*, Op. 12.

8) On 19 December he informed Breitkopf & Härtel that the title *Dichtungen* was to be replaced by 'Fantasy' (*Phantasie*). This change is reflected in the *Stichvorlage*, which contains a note from Schumann requesting that the earlier title for each movement should be replaced by a triangular device of three stars. This request was not observed when the work was published as *Fantasie*, Op. 17 in March or April 1839. As late as 20 March Schumann still referred in his diary to the 'Fantasiestücke' (*Phantasiestücke*).

Ignoring insignificant differences in spelling (*Phantasie/ Fantasie, Phantasieen/*

Phantasien) and allowing for the fact that *Phantasieen* and *Phantasiestücke* are synonymous, we are left with three different generic names for Op. 17: 'Sonata', 'Fantasies', and 'Fantasy'. Running parallel with these are a series of descriptive titles both for the work as a whole and for the individual movements: 'Obolus', incorporating 'Ruins', 'Trophies', and 'Palms'; *Fata Morgana* (Schumann mentions no separate movement titles in this instance); and 'Poems', comprising 'Ruins', 'Triumphal Arch', and 'Constellation'. The two classes of names, generic and descriptive, need to be treated separately, for they bear differently on the work. A generic name such as 'sonata' or 'fantasy' encourages us to consider the given work in relation to the tradition of similarly titled pieces. In other words, we bring to a work called 'sonata' or 'fantasy' certain expectations and assumptions derived from our knowledge of the relevant genre – knowledge which is certainly abstracted from the study of many other individual pieces. But descriptive titles arouse no such definite expectations; we might reasonably hope that a piece called *Spring Flowers* will differ musically from one called *Autumn Leaves*, but we cannot talk of a *Spring Flowers* genre against which we might hear any piece bearing that name. At the most, we may guess at the inspiration for the title and assess its appropriateness to the music at hand.

To approach the *Fantasie* via the changing generic 'claims' which Schumann made for it, then, is to take a path which will mediate between the particular and the general: between the unique form and lineaments of the work itself and the various features it shares with similarly titled works, not only by Schumann but by other composers both living and dead at the time the *Fantasie* was composed. In order to find a context for this investigation we should consider Schumann's own attitude to musical genre. This may be done by appealing not only to the works themselves but also to his copious critical writings, which were of course shaped by a particular view of musical history and a particular aesthetic stance towards the music of his own time.

Although Schumann's early piano works were frequently dismissed as eccentric and courting novelty for its own sake, he saw himself not as a modern rebel but as guardian of the tradition bequeathed by Beethoven. In his view, the way forward for composers of his generation was to cultivate the large instrumental forms which Beethoven had made so much his own.[1] Thus Schumann took a decidedly hierarchic view of musical genres; a constant theme of his criticism in the second half of the 1830s, when the *Fantasie* was composed and published, is the exhortation to eschew trifles in favour of 'higher' things. Reviewing the Rondo Scherzo, Op. 8 by Stephen Heller in 1836, for example, he praised Heller as a composer of genuine talent and promised to say more about his individuality 'when larger works appear'. In 1837, discussing the Rondino in E♭ by Vincent Lachner, he placed rondino, sonatina and sonata in ascending order of importance *en route* for the 'highest' things. And in 1839, in a review of several books of studies, Schumann suggested that this form was now exhausted, at least for the moment, and that composers should revert to 'greater art-forms, forms less seductive in their mechanical display and ostentatious bravura'.[2]

This hierarchical understanding of musical genre, proceeding from the 'small' forms such as the study up to the more elaborate, 'higher' ones like the sonata (and beyond that to orchestral genres such as the symphony), should not be taken to imply that Schumann thought the smaller ones worthless or incapable of sustaining truly artistic music. Of Ludwig Berger's Fifteen Studies, Op. 22 he wrote in 1837 that some of them 'may no longer be regarded as studies but rather belong in the first rank of art-works in the smaller genre[s]'.[3] And his high regard for Chopin's music, so much of which was cast in the 'smaller' genres, is further testimony to his view that small need not mean insignificant. A more important qualification must be entered with respect to his regard for the strictness of generic titles. While he fully understood the characteristics of the musical genres of his time, he was relatively undogmatic about generic naming in individual cases. Thus, Camill Grillparzer's Rondo in A was 'in fact no rondo, but rather a sonata[-form] movement'.[4] More arresting is Schumann's 1838 review of Schubert's Four Impromptus, Op. 142 (D. 935):

And yet I can hardly believe that Schubert really called these pieces 'Impromptus'; the first is so obviously the first movement of a sonata, is so perfectly executed and complete that there can be no doubt about it. I take the second Impromptu to be the second movement of the same sonata; it fits closely with [the first] in key and character. Schubert's friends must know what has become of the closing movements, or whether or not he finished the sonata; the fourth Impromptu might perhaps be regarded as the finale, but although the tonality supports this idea it is contradicted by the volatility of the overall structure. These are therefore mere suppositions which could only be clarified by an examination of the original manuscript. [Yet] I do not hold them unimportant; titles and headings count for little; conversely, a sonata is such a fine ornament in the garland of a composer's works that I would happily attribute another one, or even twenty, to the many by Schubert which we already have.[5]

That Schumann was quite wrong – Schubert's autograph manuscript refers to '*Vier Impromptu's*'[6] – matters less than his belief that generic titles were not always to be taken literally. Two further examples of this may be cited, both from 1839. Schumann's own *Faschingsschwank aus Wien*, Op. 26 was described on the title-page of the first edition as 'fantasy-pictures' (*Fantasiebilder*). Yet writing on 15 March to Simonin de Sire, a Belgian musical dilettante and one of his earliest admirers, Schumann called it 'a great *romantic sonata*'.[7] More interestingly, in a lengthy article reviewing the state of sonata composition in 1839 Schumann claimed that 'for the rest, however, it looks as if this form has run its course, which is indeed in the nature of things[;] we should not repeat the same thing century after century and also have an eye to the new. So, write sonatas, or fantasies (what's in a name!), only let not music be forgotten meanwhile and beg for the rest from your good genius.'[8] The association of sonata and fantasy here – the veiled implication that the terms could be interchangeable – leads directly back to the *Fantasie* destined at one stage to be called a sonata, and refocuses attention on the question of genre in this work. Is it a sonata in fantasy's clothing, or the reverse? Or is it best regarded as a series of three fantasies, the *Fantasie[e]n* of Schumann's intermediate title? The answer, as so often with Schumann, lies somewhere between all three possibilities.

Perhaps the most uncharacteristic feature of Op. 17 *qua* fantasy is its three-movement form. As a genre, the fantasy was traditionally cast as a single movement containing a number of discrete and often radically contrasting sections. Two well-known examples are Mozart's Fantasy in C minor, K. 475 and Beethoven's Op. 77. In addition to their sectional construction, both works evince the wide-ranging tonal motion typical of the genre. While the Mozart work begins and ends in C minor, and even offers a brief recapitulation of the opening material to reinforce the sense of closure, Beethoven's Op. 77 owes far more to the improvisatory 'free' fantasy associated closely with C. P. E. Bach: G minor, F minor, and Db major are touched on in quick succession at the beginning, but the piece ends with a set of variations in B major.

In this context it becomes clear that the (French) title *Fantaisie* was entirely appropriate for the first movement of Op. 17 when Schumann composed it as an independent work. That the movement was originally conceived in this way in fact serves to clarify the relationship of the *Im Legendenton* section to the whole. The traditional view, based on the application of a sonata-form paradigm, has been to read the *Im Legendenton* as a substitute development section or part thereof (see Chapter 4). If we read the movement against the generic tradition of the sectional fantasy, to which it properly belongs, we can more easily accept the *Im Legendenton* as a quasi-independent section, albeit one which is subtly linked to the two outer sections.[9] Moreover, other cases show that Schumann thought of the fantasy basically as a single-movement genre. His only other published 'fantasy' was the *Phantasie* for violin and orchestra, Op. 131, a single-movement work written in 1853. But the first movement of the Piano Concerto, Op. 54 was originally conceived as an independent piece entitled *Fantasie*; the decision to add two further movements was taken at the suggestion of the eventual publishers, Breitkopf & Härtel.[10]

In Schubert's work, however, the internal weight and construction of the individual sections developed to a point at which the fantasy came to sound more like a multi-movement work than a multi-sectional movement. The *locus classicus* for this development is the *'Wanderer' Fantasie*, D. 760, composed in 1822. Here the four sections ape the typical succession of movements in a four-movement sonata. However, none of the first three movements is tonally closed, as one would expect in a sonata proper: each runs seamlessly into the next, with the result that the work remains essentially a single movement, its overall unity further assured by the prominence of the opening material throughout.[11] For a parallel in Schumann's music we may turn to the Fourth Symphony, Op. 120, a work whose four movements play without any formal breaks and are thematically related. It is further testimony to Schumann's conception of the fantasy as a single-movement genre that he considered calling this symphony a *Symphonistische Phantasie* at one stage.[12]

The tendency for sections to aspire to the status of movements is well exemplified in Mendelssohn's *Fantasie* in F♯ minor, Op. 28, composed in 1833. Here there are only three movements, and in stark contrast to the *'Wanderer' Fantasie* they are all tonally closed. Moreover, the last two are in strict forms (Scherzo and Trio, and sonata form). To all intents and purposes the work is a piano sonata, and when he wrote it Mendelssohn at first called it *Sonate écossaise*.[13] The eventual choice of title reflects mainly on the relatively unconventional opening movement – in which the improvisatory and fantasy-like *Con moto agitato* sections contrast with the more stable Andante passages – and perhaps also on the absence of an independent slow movement. (Schumann's *Fantasie* does have a slow movement of course, but its position at the end of the work is distinctly unconventional within the sonata tradition.)

If the nineteenth-century fantasy tended to take on the multi-movement character of the piano sonata, the reverse was also true: composers tried replacing multi-movement structures with something more continuous. Favourite techniques were the avoidance or weakening of formal breaks between movements; an increasing unification of the musical material; and the recall of specific passages at different points to create a cyclic effect. Another work by Mendelssohn, the Sonata in E, Op. 6 of 1826, is a good example.

Indeed, the way in which the closing passage from the end of the first movement returns at the end of the finale foreshadows Schumann's aborted plan to end the third movement of the *Fantasie* in the same way.

Schumann may have been the first critic to note the resemblance between the first movement of Mendelssohn's Op. 6 and that of Beethoven's Piano Sonata in A, Op. 101;[14] and it is Beethoven's music which provides the most distinguished examples of the piano sonata-as-fantasy. His interest in a *rapprochement* between the two genres is evident as early as the two Op. 27 sonatas, in E♭ major and C♯ minor, which were published as *Sonata quasi una fantasia*. Here again, the fantasy element in the title seems above all to reflect Beethoven's rejection of the conventional sonata-allegro model for the opening movement. Op. 27 No. 1 is the more unusual of the two works in that the *Attacca subito* directions cause the distinction between one movement and the next to blur. This sonata, like the sectional fantasy, plays as a continuous whole.[15] And although he never used the particular title again, *quasi una fantasia* is an apt description for a number of the later sonatas. Op. 101, for example, exhibits a number of the characteristics mentioned above. The nature and order of the movements is unconventional. The unusually unassertive first movement is almost crushed by the following march, which, with its obsessive dotted rhythms, cannot have been far from Schumann's mind when he was writing the second-movement march in the *Fantasie*. Following the march, the slow, relatively amorphous *Adagio, ma non troppo, con affetto* section – one hesitates to call it a 'movement' – dissolves into a recall of the beginning of the first movement, which itself gives way without a break to the finale.

A companion piece to Op. 101 is the contemporaneous Cello Sonata in C, Op. 102 No. 1. This falls into two broad sections, the first comprising the tonic-key Andante and ensuing Allegro vivace in the unexpected key of A minor, the relative minor. The second half plays continuously, with a 'free fantasy'-like Adagio passage leading into a return of the Andante prior to the finale. Significantly, Beethoven described Op. 102 No. 1 as a 'free sonata' (*freje Sonate*) in the autograph score. And the last three piano sonatas, Op. 109–11, further illustrate his interest in joining movements together to form larger units as well as in relating movements to one another in various ways. His most radical attempt in applying these techniques, though, must be reckoned as the String Quartet in C♯ minor, Op. 131, the seven movements (actually numbered as sections in the score) of which are all carefully linked one to the next while the transformed return of the opening fugue theme in the finale gives a palpable cyclic cohesion to the whole.[16]

Examined against this background of sonata-fantasies and fantasy-sonatas, the organization of the *Fantasie* is remarkably clear: three substantial movements, each closing firmly in its own tonic key. There is none of the open-endedness associated with the Beethoven works just discussed, and which is such a characteristic feature of much of Schumann's other piano music from the 1830s. Schumann even denied us the opportunity to enjoy a cyclic structure by suppressing his proposed recall of the first-movement ending at the close of the finale. Also significant is the fact that in contrast to Beethoven's tendency to shift the expected weighty sonata-allegro movement from first to last place in his 'fantasy' works, the weightiest movement in the *Fantasie* is undoubtedly the first. All these features suggest that the *Fantasie* is closer to the sonata than to the genre announced by its title.[17]

Conversely, other considerations militate against the *Fantasie*-as-sonata. Although Schumann was well aware of the fluid number of movements in the late Beethoven sonata – four in Op. 106, three in Op. 109, two in Op. 111 – he seems to have regarded four as the norm, one to which he adhered rather closely. This is reflected both in his writing about and his writing of sonatas. After suggesting that the first, second and fourth of Schubert's Impromptus, D. 935 were really the corresponding movements of a piano sonata (Schumann had only harsh words for the popular third piece in the set), he went so far as to say that one might perform the three in that order 'and then you will have, *if not a complete sonata*, at least one further beautiful remembrance of the man'.[18] His own Sonatas in F♯ minor and G minor, Op. 11 and 22 each have four movements, with the slow movement placed second and the scherzo third. The slow movement is the only one not in the tonic key (A, the relative major, in Op. 11; C, the major subdominant, in Op. 22). Moreover, the weighting of the movements conforms to tradition, in that two large-scale and relatively complex outer movements frame two smaller and lighter ones in each case. Sonata form is used in the first movement of each, with even such niceties as a repeated exposition being observed.

That Schumann was not entirely inflexible in his approach to the sonata is shown by his third published work in the genre. Certainly, his *Troisième grande sonate*, published in 1853, corresponds closely to the pattern of Opp. 11 and 22: four movements, with the scherzo (in the submediant, D♭ major) placed second and the tonic-key slow movement third. The original version, written in summer 1836, included a second scherzo, but neither was included in the first publication of the work as the three-movement *Concert sans orchestre*, Op. 14. Even in its original five-movement form, however, the sequence and character of the movements in Op. 14 conform more closely to sonata tradition than do the three movements of the contemporary *Fantasie*.[19] As his friend and first biographer Wilhelm Joseph von Wasielewski pointed out (see Chapter 4), all three movements of the *Fantasie* draw to some extent upon the formal conventions of sonata form, although their sequence is quite uncharacteristic of the genre. The sequence might be explained with reference to late Beethoven: it is as if Schumann has borrowed the idea of a second-movement march from the A major Sonata, Op. 101 and that of a gentle concluding movement from Opp. 109 and 111, though Schumann's third movement is formally remote from the variation sets which end these two Beethoven works.

So there is reason to think that Schumann would not have thought of the *Fantasie* as a sonata in the sense in which he normally understood the latter term. But as he himself reminds us, 'what's in a name?' The review of the Schubert Impromptus dates from 1838. An earlier review, this time from the year in which the *Fantasie* was composed, bears on that work in an especially interesting way. Reviewing Julie Baroni-Cavalcabò's *Bravour-Allegro*, Op. 8 in 1836, Schumann observed that the piece was essentially in first-movement sonata form ('excepting the missing development section') and suggested that *two* further movements should be added to create a piano sonata, since the publication of a work in this genre would enhance the composer's reputation.[20] Schumann might almost have been describing the genesis of the *Fantasie* here. To his independently composed *Fantaisie* of June 1836, itself by no means in standard sonata-allegro form, he had added two further movements and then offered the whole to Kistner as a 'sonata for Beethoven'. Quite apart from his concern to enhance his own reputation as a composer, Schumann's choice of genre-title on this occasion probably had far more to do with the intended purpose and dedication of the work than with its internal characteristics.[21]

In assessing the *Fantasie* in relation to the genres of fantasy and sonata the issues are relatively clear-cut. Each genre can be clearly defined, even if we have to deal with a certain amount of cross-fertilization. But Schumann's third generic title, *Fantasie[e]n* or *Fantasiestücke*, resists such precise definition. To think of the *Fantasie* in this way is to align it with numerous works by Schumann bearing related titles: the *Fantasiestücke*, Op. 12, composed in 1837 and from which Schumann particularly wished to distinguish the *Fantasie* by the title *Dichtungen*; the *Fantasiestücke*, Op. 73 for clarinet and piano (1849); the *Phantasiestücke*, Op. 88 for violin, cello, and piano (1842); and the *Fantasiestücke*, Op. 111 for piano (1851). In addition, there is *Kreisleriana*, Op. 16, subtitled *Fantasien für Pianoforte* (1838), and also that 'great romantic sonata', the *Faschingsschwank aus Wien*, Op. 26 (1839–40), subtitled *Fantasiebilder* ('fantasy-pictures'). Another work falling into the same category is the *Nachtstücke*, Op. 23 (1839), which Schumann originally intended to call *Leichenphantasie* ('Corpse-fantasy').[22]

It is difficult to establish precise criteria for a work called *Fantasiestücke* or *Fantasien* beyond the rather obvious point that it will consist of a number of individual pieces. How many pieces is unclear: Schumann's Op. 12 consists of two 'books' (*Hefte*) each containing four pieces; *Kreisleriana* is made up of eight pieces but without any subdivision; Op. 88 consists of four pieces, Op. 111 of three. Nor is there any obvious consensus about individual length or form in these works. Another issue concerns interrelationships between the pieces in a set. There are fairly palpable connections between the openings of the first two *Nachtstücke* in Op. 23, for example, but it is by no means obvious whether, to what extent, or in what way the pieces in Op. 12 or *Kreisleriana* are interconnected. A brief glance at several works shows that overall tonal plan may or may not be a feature. The four Op. 88 pieces have the key scheme a–F–d–a/A. Both outer pieces in Op. 111 are in C minor while the central piece is in A♭, the submediant of that key. The *Faschingsschwank* could be said to be 'in' B♭ since its first, third, and final movements are in that key and the second and fourth are in the related minor keys of G and E♭. On the other hand, *Kreisleriana* and the *Fantasiestücke*, Op. 12 display no such obvious – indeed, such sonata-like – overall tonal schemes.

In short, it is unclear whether large tonal schemes or inter-movement relationships are necessary characteristics of a work called *Fantasiestücke* or some similar title. Nor is it always clear that these are indeed 'works', as opposed to collections of smaller works. Must the eight pieces in *Kreisleriana* always be performed as a totality? Is their ordering sacrosanct, or may the pieces be rearranged? These are pressing questions which have hardly begun to be tackled.[23] The *attacca* links between the three pieces in Op. 111 and the title *Finale* for the last piece in Op. 88 are obvious pointers toward the indivisibility of these works; yet Schumann was happy for Clara to play only selected pieces from the *Fantasiestücke*, Op.12.[24] Thus the complex interrelationships between the three movements of the *Fantasie* (see Chapter 5) and its overall key scheme C–E♭–C have no real bearing on the appropriateness or otherwise of Schumann's titles *Fantasien* and *Fantasiestücke*. And although it is now customary to regard the *Fantasie* as an indivisible whole, Chapter 6 will suggest that performances of individual movements were not uncommon in the nineteenth century.

Finally, there are the descriptive titles which Schumann considered attaching to the *Fantasie*. He told Simonin de Sire in his letter of 15 March 1839 that the titles of his compositions always occurred to him after the music had been written, and there is no reason to suppose that this was not also the case with the first set of titles given to the *Fantasie*: *Ruinen, Trophäen, Palmen*, the whole work to be called *Obolus auf Beethovens Denkmal*. As has been argued in Chapter 1, the first-movement title *Ruinen* (originally the French *Ruines*) must have had strong autobiographical resonances for Schumann, reminding him of his complete separation from Clara in the summer of 1836. The titles for the other two movements have straightforward heroic connections and seem easily warranted by the intended purpose of the work at this stage. The importance to Schumann of the title *Ruinen* is clear, since it alone was retained when in 1838 he renamed the other two movements *Siegesbogen* and *Sternbild* and called the whole work *Dichtungen*. A possible explanation for this last name will emerge at the end of Chapter 3; as for *Siegesbogen*, this seems to continue the Beethovenian association (is it coincidental that the second movement of the *Fantasie* shares its tonic key with the 'Eroica' Symphony?), while the choice of *Sternbild* for the third movement is harder to explain in terms of any concrete association.

The most intriguing name of all is *Fata Morgana*, the title for the *Phantasieen* which Schumann put to Breitkopf & Härtel on 6 February 1838. It appears never to have been noticed in the literature on the *Fantasie*, and was not associated with separate titles for the individual movements. The term itself refers to a mirage associated particularly with Sicily and popularly believed to be caused by the magical workings of the 'Fairy Morgana'. It appears to have entered the German language in the late eighteenth century, and is found in the writings of authors such as Wieland and Goethe. It even appears, although in German rather than Latin form, in Jean Paul's *Flegeljahre*, a text which one immediately associates with Schumann.[25] However, it was probably another, much less well-known source from which Schumann took his inspiration in this case. In his diary for 14 January 1838 he noted that he had derived great satisfaction from reading Hermann von Pückler-Muskau's *Semilasso in Africa*.[26] This book, telling of the author's travels in Africa, contains two episodes in which he sees a mirage or (as he calls it on the second occasion) *fata morgana*.[27] Surely it was Schumann's excited response to these episodes which, only weeks after reading the book, suggested the title *Fata Morgana* for his *Phantasieen*. It is easy to imagine how much the illusory quality of the mirage would have appealed to him; by 1838 the sorry events which two years earlier had inspired particularly the first movement of the *Fantasie* may have come to seem unreal and mirage-like themselves.

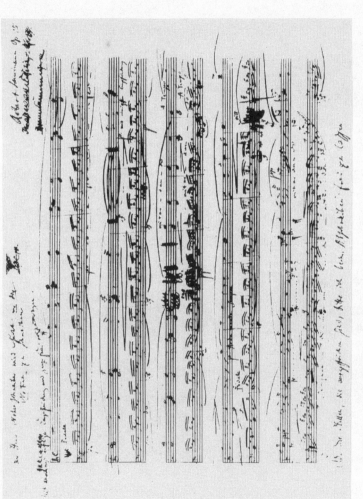

Plate 1. *Fantasie*, first movement, bars 1–29. Schumann's autograph manuscript (present location unknown). © Sotheby's. Reproduced by permission of Sotheby's and the Syndics of Cambridge University Library

Plate 2. *Fantasie*, first movement, bars 125–66. Schumann's autograph manuscript (present location unknown). © Sotheby's. Reproduced by permission of Sotheby's and the Syndics of Cambridge University Library

Fata Morgana was superseded by *Dichtungen, Dichtungen* by *Fantasie*; but the mirage continued to hold Schumann's gaze a little longer. In November 1838 he noted in his diary that he had had 'ideas for a *Fata Morgana* for Clara'.[28] This little piece was eventually published as *Vision* in the *Albumblätter*, Op. 124. Musically it bears no relation to the *Fantasie*, nor does its printed title hint at any relationship to the genesis of that much larger work. But we know now that 'what's in a name' may be a good deal more than meets the eye.

3

Allusion and quotation in the 'Fantasie'

Schumann's early piano works abound in allusion. Broadly speaking, the allusion may be of two kinds: a work may allude to other musical works, whether of Schumann or another composer; or the allusion may be to non-musical material, in which case we may speak of an extra-musical meaning enshrined in the work by means of allusion. An example of the former type is the appearance in *Florestan* from *Carnaval* of the theme from *Papillons* No. 1 (the theme also plays an important part in the finale of that work). By quoting quite literally from the earlier work here, Schumann alludes more generally to it as a whole: *Papillons* is imported into *Carnaval*. As examples of extra-musical allusion we might take the verbal references to the dying away of the noise of carnival night ('Das Geräusch der Faschingsnacht verstummt') and to the striking of the clock ('Die Thurmuhr schlägt sechs') written into the finale of *Papillons*, a movement which is based closely on a scene from Jean Paul's novel *Flegeljahre* and which alludes musically to the *Grossvatertanz* traditionally played at the end of balls.[1] The extra-musical meaning of the 'Sphinx' motives A♭–C–B and A–E♭–C–B on which *Carnaval* is largely based resides in their being the 'musical' letters in Schumann's surname and also a 'spelling' of ASCH, the birthplace of Ernestine von Fricken, to whom he was briefly engaged. (B is called *H* in German, while A♭ is *As* and E♭ is *Es*, pronounced like 'S'.)

The *Fantasie*, and especially its first movement, is rich in allusions of various kinds. Before pursuing these the distinction between 'allusion' and 'quotation' hinted at above must be further explored. Both are forms of reference, means of bringing into a work material which exists independently of the work itself. Quotation is usually thought of as stronger than allusion; a quotation is often explicitly identified, and meant to be recognized by its audience. Allusion, on the other hand, is reference of a more covert kind. Although allusions may be made as self-consciously as quotations, they are not always intended to be so clearly recognized: much of their allure lies in the fact that they refer obliquely, and partly obscure their sources. Nor is the 'reality' of an allusion

Example 3.1a: Beethoven, *An die ferne Geliebte*, bars 266–7 (Song VI)

Nimm sie hin denn, die- se Lie- der,

Example 3.1b: Schumann, *Fantasie*, first movement, bars 295–7

necessarily dependent on its being consciously intended: a work may allude or even quote behind its author's back, so to speak. Schumann took pleasure in this, as is clear from an amusing exchange of letters with Clara late in 1839. On 25 November Clara jokingly described Schumann as a 'musical thief', saying that she had recognized in Beethoven's 'Hammerklavier' Sonata a passage which Schumann had used in one of his own works. Schumann, replying on 1 December, recognized his 'theft' in the opening of a sonata in B♭ which he had often played to Clara assuming that she would know what it was, 'but which I have not had published. Sillyhead! If I steal, I begin much more subtly, as you yourself know from your own experience – namely with your heart.' Clara riposted on 3 December that she was well aware of the quotation Schumann mentioned; she had been referring to a 'theft' from the middle of the Beethoven work, 'so that it's hardly noticed.' Schumann's reply, on 8 December, was to say, 'I'm looking forward to [being shown] the Beethoven theft! . . . I must say that I'm pleased when I discover anything like that in my compositions.'[2]

The distinction between quotation and allusion is relevant to the first movement of the *Fantasie*, which is often said to contain a quotation from the last song in Beethoven's cycle *An die ferne Geliebte*.[3] Beethoven's phrase, transposed from E♭ to C, is given in Example 3.1a and Schumann's supposed quotation in Example 3.1b. In spite of the similarities, significant differences are apparent. Schumann's melodic line follows Beethoven's very closely, but it is given a different rhythmic and harmonic setting and there is no reference whatever to Beethoven's accompanimental figure.

Quotation or allusion? The latter term is more appropriate in view of the veiled quality of the reference, if reference it is. For there is no certainty that Schumann *was* alluding to the Beethoven work here: the connection appears first to have been made as late as 1910, in the second edition of Hermann Abert's book on Schumann.[4] Ironically, Schumann did admit to a different Beethoven quotation in the *Fantasie*. In his letter to Kistner dated 19 December 1836 he wrote that 'In the "Palms" [the third movement] there is a quotation from the Adagio of the A major Symphony.' Abert made no mention of the letter or the quotation, but in 1904 Gustav Jansen suggested that a 'faint echo' of the Allegretto of the symphony was to be heard in the *Fantasie*, in the bass rhythm in bars 30–3 and 87–90 of the third movement (see Example 3.2a–b).[5] The 'echo' might seem fortuitous (and the point dubious) had not Schumann already used the same Beethoven theme in 1833 as the basis of a set of piano variations, his posthumously published *Etuden in Form freier Variationen über ein Beethovensches Thema*. Generally, however, when Schumann's remark to Kistner has been noted at all it has been assumed that the quotation from the symphony was excised in Schumann's supposed revisions to the *Fantasie* between its composition in 1836 and its publication in 1839.[6]

In any case, that Schumann did not admit to a reference to *An die ferne Geliebte* in the first movement of the *Fantasie* in no way excludes the possibility that he was well aware of one. There are compelling reasons why such an allusion would have been especially meaningful. As we know, Schumann described the first movement of the *Fantasie* as 'a deep lament' for Clara; it was composed at a time when the lovers were completely separated, unable to take comfort even from an occasional exchange of letters. The whole subject of Beethoven's cycle is of course the 'distant beloved', and in the last song the poet suggests that by singing the songs which he has sung, his beloved will lessen the distance between them. It is precisely the music set to the words 'Take them then, these songs' ('Nim[m] sie hin denn diese Lieder') which is

Example 3.2

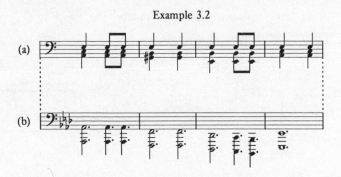

(a) Beethoven, Seventh Symphony, second movement, bars 3–6
(b) Schumann, *Fantasie*, third movement, bars 30–3

alluded to in bars 295–7 of the *Fantasie*. Given its autobiographical suitability, it is difficult to believe that the allusion was not consciously intended. And Schumann's plan to recall the ending of the first movement at the end of the third (see Chapter 1), by drawing further attention to the allusive passage, increases the suspicion that it had a special significance for him. We might even speak of a planned double allusion here, for Schumann must have known that the last verse of the final song of *An die ferne Geliebte* recalls both the music and text of the corresponding verse in the first song.

If the reference to *An die ferne Geliebte* is best termed an allusion, there is no question that the four-line 'motto' at the head of the *Fantasie* is a direct and literal quotation from Friedrich Schlegel, whose name is even printed underneath. The quotation comes from *Die Gebüsche* ('The Bushes'), which forms part of a cycle of poems called *Abendröte* ('Sunset'). The cycle consists of two parts each containing ten poems and preceded by an untitled prologue; *Die Gebüsche* is the ninth poem of the second part, and Schumann's motto consists of its final quatrain.[7] Many commentators have understandably drawn attention to Schumann's letter of 9 June 1839 to Clara in which he suggests that she is the *leiser Ton* of the motto. Yet read in its proper context the remark loses much of its evidential authority. As suggested in Chapter 1, Schumann was responding to Clara's punning allusions to the motto in her earlier letter of 22 May, in which she acknowledged receipt of the *Fantasie* and gave her initial reaction to it. Clara referred to Schumann's own 'notes' (*Töne*); he, in his turn, was making a reciprocal link between Clara and Schlegel's *Ton*. All this seems more a playful exchange of word play than a serious discussion of

Example 3.3: Schumann, *Fantasie*, third movement, bars 1–11

the 'inner meaning' of the motto, the more so in view of the relatively late appearance of the motto as an element in the work: while there is no doubt that the distant Clara was a very real 'presence' in the composition of the first movement in 1836, the motto first appears only in the *Stichvorlage* of 1838.

Other ramifications of the motto are pertinent in the context of a discussion of allusion and quotation. At the end of Chapter 1 it was suggested that Schumann came across Schlegel's *Abendröte* around February 1838, when he was preparing the *Fantasie* (at that stage called *Dichtungen*) for dispatch to Breitkopf & Härtel. The appearance in the *NZfM* of a quotation from Schlegel's poem *Bündnis* shows that he had some contact with Schlegel's poetry during that period. If we may suppose that he had been browsing

Example 3.4: Schubert, *'Wanderer' Fantasie*, bars 1–20

through the poems at some length, he can hardly have failed to notice a striking allusion between his chosen quotation from *Abendröte*, beginning 'Durch alle Töne tönet' and the opening line of another poem, 'Alte Töne tönen wieder' ('Old notes resound again'). The poem, with its images of the sorrows and joys of love, would surely have moved Schumann, and in 1838 its final lines must have seemed especially pertinent to his and Clara's situation:

Alles kann der Mut besiegen,	Courage can conquer everything,
Mut entsprungen hohem Glauben;	Courage sprung from deep faith;
Keiner kann die Liebe rauben,	No one can steal love,
Wie auch wechseln die Gefühle	However much feelings change
In dem irdischen Gewühle.	In the throng of mortal life.

The title of this poem, with its allusive reference to Schumann's motto, is none other than *Fantasie*.[8]

There is a further possible connection between Schumann's *Fantasie* and Schlegel's *Die Gebüsche*. Schlegel's *leiser Ton* is just one of three instances in the poem (which is only sixteen lines long) in which the adjective or adverb *leise* ('soft, gentle') is used.[9] Although it may be no more than a fortuitous coincidence, it is interesting that in revising the *Stichvorlage* early in 1838 Schumann changed the original instruction *Einfach und getragen* ('simple and solemn') at the head of the third movement to *Langsam getragen[.] Durchweg leise zu halten* ('Slow and solemn. To be kept soft throughout'). Conversely, it is unfortunate that what initially seems a much more compelling allusion involving the opening of the third movement must be relegated to the realms of the coincidental, if serendipitous. Schubert set no fewer than ten of the poems from Schlegel's *Abendröte*, including *Die Gebüsche* (D. 646). It has been observed that 'the undulating sextuplet accompanimental figure that runs through Schubert's setting is called up in the last movement of Schumann's *Fantasie*, which, in addition, begins with a variant of the harmonic progression that opens Schubert's song'.[10] At face value, the relationship is close enough to describe the opening of the Schumann movement as a direct quotation of Schubert's song. But the connection falters since Schubert's *Die Gebüsche*, composed in January 1819, was not published until 1885. While it is conceivable that Schumann might have known it from a manuscript copy, it must be more likely that he was quite unaware of the song.[11]

This does not exhaust the possible allusions to Schubert embedded within the third movement of the *Fantasie*, however. One important function of genre, discussed in Chapter 2, is to set up an allusive network. That is, simply by calling a work 'fantasy' the composer is alluding to a particular generic tradition against which we are invited to 'read' his composition. In this sense, the work alludes to all others bearing the same title. In the case of the *Fantasie*, one work in the tradition stands out particularly starkly: Schubert's *'Wanderer' Fantasie*. Published in 1823, this shares not only its generic title with the *Fantasie* but also its large-scale, multi-'movement' form and its overall key. Beyond all this, there is a much more specific allusion to be heard at the beginning of Schumann's third movement. After a four-bar introduction, a

Example 3.5: Schubert, *An die Musik*, bars 17–19 (cf. Example 3.1b)

in ei- ne bess'- re Welt ent- rückt.

theme is introduced in the middle voice above a stepwise descending bass. Beginning in the tonic, the phrase cadences on the dominant of A minor in bar 6. A second, more extended phrase cadences on the same chord in bar 10, and after a pause there is a return to the tonic and what sounds like a second beginning which now continues differently (Example 3.3).

All of this takes place in a hushed context and a slow tempo: the contrast between Schumann's *Langsam getragen*[.] *Durchweg leise zu halten* and Schubert's *fortissimo* opening, *Allegro con fuoco ma non troppo*, could hardly be greater. Yet further inspection reveals a close relationship. There is no introductory passage in the *'Wanderer'*, but Schumann's opening bar presents an arpeggiated form of precisely the chord with which Schubert's wanderings begin. And after opening in the tonic, Schubert's first paragraph comes to rest on the dominant of A minor in bar 17. Following a half-bar's rest extended by a pause there is a second beginning which, just as in the Schumann movement, continues differently (Example 3.4). Even the details of Schubert's cadence in bars 14–17 are closely matched at the end of Schumann's first phrase in bar 6.[12] Rather than speaking of allusion here, it might be more appropriate to frame the relationship between these opening strategies as one of intertextuality.[13]

Finally, it is an allusion to another Schubert song, albeit not one of those from the *Abendröte* sequence, which returns us to the first movement of the *Fantasie* and to Schumann's music as opposed to Schlegel's motto. In his letter to von Zuccalmaglio dated 2 July 1836, Schumann claimed that only music had been able to lift him out of the depths of despair to which he had recently sunk: it was music which had given him back his strength and courage. He would have been aware of the similar claims for the power of music made in Franz von Schober's poem *An die Musik*, which Schubert had set in 1817:[14]

41

Du holde Kunst,	O blessed art,
in wieviel grauen Stunden,	how often in dark hours,
Wo mich des Lebens	When I am trapped
wilder Kreis umstrickt,	in life's frenzied round,
Hast du mein Herz	Have you kindled warm love
zu warmer Lieb entzunden,	in my heart,
Hast mich in eine bess're Welt	Have transported me
entrückt!	to a better world!

Listening again to bars 295–6 of the first movement of the *Fantasie*, one is struck by the extent to which the melodic line and (more importantly) the harmony conjure up Schubert's invocation of a 'better world' or (in verse 2 of the song) the 'blessed art' of music which transports the poet to that world: Example 3.5, which shows bars 17–19 of *An die Musik* transposed to C, should be compared with the Schumann passage already quoted in Example 3.1b. Thus the allusive quality of this celebrated passage in the *Fantasie* is richer than has normally been supposed: Schumann appears to evoke two appeals to the power of music celebrated by two of his most revered predecessors. In Beethoven's case, it is music's power to bridge the distance between the poet and his beloved; in Schubert's, its power to transcend the ephemeral world and its pressures. In June 1836 Schumann drew on music to both these ends. And given the web of allusions and quotations, both musical and literary, embedded in the *Fantasie*, it seems only appropriate that after much searching he should have hit upon the title *Dichtungen* ('Poems'): as he explained to Clara on 16 April 1838 (see Chapter 1), it was 'a very noble and significant term for musical compositions'.

4

Form in the first movement

Form and sonata form

To speak of such a movement as a sonata form with irregularities is like calling a dog irregular when it grows long whiskers, washes its face, and miaows.[1]

Viewed individually – their sequence is obviously unconventional – all three movements appear at first to be somewhat akin to sonata form; only upon closer acquaintance does one realize that a characteristic element in the *Fantasie* is precisely the free mixture of different art forms.[2]

As regards form, the mistake comes in wanting to claim that the [first movement] is in any *single* form.[3]

The first of these three statements wryly anticipates one of the main conclusions reached below. And to juxtapose the other two, published in 1858 and 1984 respectively, is in a sense to summarize the history of attempts to analyse the first movement of the *Fantasie* while demonstrating how circular that history has been. The first movement has always been recognized as the most distinguished of the three. This tradition stems from Schumann himself, who described the movement to Clara as the most passionate piece he had ever written. As for the issue of form, analysts have been much exercised by the relationship to the whole of the *Im Legendenton* section. To the extent that this separately titled section is in a different key, metre and tempo to the rest of the movement, it appears to form an independent interlude; but closer study reveals that it grows out of the preceding music. It is precisely this quality of ambiguity, the capacity to bear multiple meanings, which distinguishes so much of the material of the first movement and makes it such a rich and fascinating – yet problematic – object of study.

To attempt as neutral an account as possible, a listener coming to this movement for the first time would almost certainly be aware of three large sections: bars 1–128; bars 129–224 (the *Im Legendenton*); and bars 225–309. Furthermore, there would be a fairly obvious resemblance between the last section and a large portion of the first. To be more specific, the whole of the last section up to bar 291 runs parallel with bars 29 (plus upbeat)–102 in the first section.[4] The main differences are the omission of bars 37–40 and the associated ensuing transposition of the music in the third section. Bar 232, corresponding to 36, leads into bar 233, which however corresponds to bar 41. Starting from the second beat of bar 233, all the material of the first section is repeated one tone lower than at its original presentation. This level of transposition persists until bar 279, where a second omission occurs. This time the transition from bar 278 to 279 represents a cut from bar 86 directly to bar 90, with the material from bar 90 onward now being transposed down a fifth.[5] The transposition ceases at bar 286, however, for at this point the material of bars 97–102 reappears at its original pitch, introduced this time by G rather than D in the bass. Already there is a complication here, for bars 97–105 themselves correspond to a much earlier passage, bars 19–28. Thus bars 286–91 of the third section have not one but two referents in the first section. To put it another way: we can hear bars 285–6 either as parallel to bars 96–7 – an analysis which is supported by the much larger correspondence between the third section as a whole and bars 29–102 in the first section; or, on the other hand, we may hear the move from bar 285 to 286 as equivalent to one from bar 96 back to bar 19.

It is the unmistakable three-part structure and the nature of the relationship between the first and third sections which inevitably suggest a sonata-form paradigm for the movement. Yet a brief survey of some of the accounts which assume that paradigm suffices to reveal its inadequacy here. Indeed, the very vagueness of many accounts – the lack of precise bar-references, for example – is probably symptomatic of their authors' uneasiness with a Classical model which ill fits the *Fantasie* in many respects but seems unavoidable in view of Schumann's strong awareness of the Classical tradition and the generic expectations set up by the three-movement sonata-like structure of the *Fantasie* as a whole.

For Wasielewski, writing in 1858, the paradigm applied most neatly to the first section:

Thus the character of the first section in the first movement, which develops essentially from the main idea that runs to bar 19, is unmistakably that of sonata form; then there follows a development in song form which is only once interrupted by the passing entry of the main theme [of the first section], and finally the first section reappears slightly modified.[6]

Implicit here is the assumption that the first section functions as a sonata-form exposition. But Wasielewski fought shy of identifying such details as the location of the transition from a first to a second subject group, or even the existence of a second group at all. Indeed, his reference to a 'passing entry of the main theme' in the middle section is curious in that he seems to be referring to bars 181–94 of the *Im Legendenton*, where, however, the theme recalled from the first section is one that most commentators identify precisely with the second rather than the first subject group.

Walter Dahms, writing in 1916, invoked 'the form of the Beethovenian fantasy-sonata' (that is, the *sonata quasi una fantasia* of Beethoven's Op. 27) in connection with the *Fantasie*; yet despite this broader approach he was more specific in his use of sonata-form terminology than Wasielewski. Like the latter, he regarded bars 1–19 as the main theme (*Hauptthema*), and identified as a 'second subject' (*Seitenthema*) the melody which enters in bar 41. Unlike Wasielewski, Dahms did not explicitly identify the *Im Legendenton* as a development section, but he did characterize the third section as a 'free recapitulation' (*freie Reprise*).[7]

Joan Chissell's book on Schumann, first published in 1948 and several times revised, presents a slightly different view again. Most surprising here is the apparent identification of the middle-voice theme in bar 33 as the beginning of the second group:

such was [Schumann's] ardour in this rhapsodic first movement that exposition, development and recapitulation, like the themes themselves, flow into each other. Moreover, despite the lyrical nature of the subject matter, the central section brings true, organic development, notably when the second subject's initial uprising fourth grows into a grave C minor episode headed *Im Legendenton*.[8]

Chissell's later book on Schumann's piano works is even more explicit in certain respects: the first movement of the *Fantasie* is 'the most masterly of all his keyboard arguments in sonata form'; 'the exposition is not repeated'. Most significant is the identification of the *Im Legendenton* as an 'episode' which occurs 'in the course of the development' – but we are not told exactly where the development begins in Chissell's reading.[9]

Yonty Solomon's account, published in the same year as these latter remarks by Chissell, places a good deal of faith in the sonata-form analogy:

Structurally, the first movement falls into the three main sections of sonata form. Here the Development corresponds to the C minor episode marked 'Im Legendenton' . . . This idea has been skilfully metamorphosed from a subsidiary theme in the Exposition, and is not the 'new episode' it sounds at first . . . As for the Recapitulation, this appears to begin daringly in the 'wrong' key of E♭ major . . . But when we examine the structure more carefully, we see that Schumann has merely by-passed his opening pages and come in at a later stage of the main idea. The 'missing' stage turns up in the coda.[10]

More recently, John Daverio has argued for yet another way in which the outlines of classical sonata form may be discerned in the first movement of the *Fantasie*. In his view there is a threefold presentation of the first-group material, in C and E♭ major, in bars 1–32. The transition 'is under way' by bar 33, and the 'second theme group', which likewise combines two third-related keys (D minor and F major), occupies bars 41–81.[11] The most original aspect of Daverio's reading, however, is his identification of the *Im Legendenton* not as the development section or even an episode within that section, but as an interlude within the recapitulation:

Although the *Im Tempo* at m[easure] 82 commences with all the rhetorical posturing and tonal instability of a development section, it soon becomes clear that this was just so much false motion; with the reappearance of a variant of the opening material at its original pitch level (m. 97), the recapitulation is already under way.[12]

A beguiling idea, not least because of Daverio's shrewd observation that the bars either side of the *Im Legendenton* correspond to bars 27–9 in the exposition, and that *Im Legendenton* must therefore fall within the recapitulation.[13] But even this position has been challenged by Anthony Newcomb, who agrees with Daverio's analysis up to the beginning of the development at bar 82, but argues that the 'relative size and weight of events' up to this point in the movement is such as to render premature a recapitulation beginning as early as bar 97; this would make the development section far too short.[14]

Thus the application of a sonata-form paradigm to the first movement of the *Fantasie* is by no means straightforward: the most that might be salvaged from the foregoing is the conclusion that principles of sonata form are operative in the movement, although to an extent which resists precise definition. Leaving aside such matters as the location of the beginning of the second group, the crucial issue clearly seems to be the role of the *Im Legendenton*. Does it act as the development section of a (relatively) conventional sonata form? Does it form an interlude or episode within such a section? Or does it function as an interlude or episode within a sonata-form recapitulation, as Daverio would have it?

The first of these questions is the most easily answered. Whoever wishes to claim that the three sections of this movement correspond to the conventional exposition–development–recapitulation schema of sonata form must confront the fact that Schumann's handling of tonality runs entirely counter to the requirements of the paradigm. The exposition of a major-key sonata form normally sets up what Charles Rosen has termed a 'polarization or opposition' between the tonic and dominant (or substitute dominant) keys. 'The essential character of this opposition may be defined as a large-scale dissonance: the material played outside the tonic (i.e., in the second group) is dissonant with respect to the center of stability, or tonic.' The resolution of the large-scale dissonance comes in the recapitulation, where material heard *outside* the tonic in the exposition is recapitulated *in* the tonic: 'the principle of *recapitulation as resolution* may be considered the most fundamental and radical innovation of sonata style'.[15] In the first movement of the *Fantasie* the polarization set up in the 'exposition' involves a weakly defined C major tonic and the D minor/F major pairing of the second group: a 'flatward' tonal move quite at odds with the Classical 'sharpward' rise to the dominant. Moreover, the expected return to the tonic at the beginning of the recapitulation is wholly omitted, and the second group reappears in C minor/Eb major.[16]

It is useful to think more generally of sonata-form structure in terms of a distinction between *stability* and *instability*. That is, the recapitulation is more stable than the exposition, in that it is free from the tonal polarity developed there. Similarly, exposition and recapitulation are both more stable than the development, the tonal events of which are the least predictable of all.[17] Tonal stability and instability tend to be matched in the thematic or melodic organization: the exposition and recapitulation generally present stable, identifiable thematic units which are fragmented – rendered unstable – in the development.

The problem with the *Im Legendenton*, if we wish to regard it as a development, is that it does not at all conform to these criteria. Far from being unstable, it is the most tonally stable and unified of the three sections, being firmly rooted in the tonic minor. After a four-bar introduction, the main theme is stated unambiguously in C minor in bars 133–9. Nor is there any doubt about the prevailing C minor at the end of the section (bars 216–24), where an essentially new melodic idea accompanies the straightforward cadential progression in the bass. It is only after the main theme has appeared again in C minor in bars 174–80 that the music departs significantly from the orbit of this key, moving up a semitone to Db for the introduction of the theme heard previously in bars 41–7 and 61–8, in the keys of D minor and F major.[18] This is Wasielewski's equivocal 'passing entry of the main theme'; and inasmuch as they present a significant 'exposition' theme in a 'remote' or 'foreign' key, bars 181–94 could be considered the only conventionally developmental bars in this section. Against this one might set Chissell's point that 'true, organic development' is offered in the transformation of the theme heard in bars 33–7 into the main theme of the *Im Legendenton*. On the contrary,

Example 4.1: first movement, bars 28, 82–3

however, it is precisely the presence of a 'main theme' here at all which weakens the claim for a true sonata-form development. The *Im Legendenton* is far too stable, both tonally and thematically, to fulfil such a role. A further important consequence of its closed, inward-looking nature is that it does not prepare the recapitulation in any real sense. In a conventional sonata-form movement, the ultimate tonal goal of the development lies beyond it, in the return of the tonic key at the beginning of the recapitulation. The end of the *Im Legendenton* is complete in itself.

The second and third questions may be answered together. Whether we choose to hear the *Im Legendenton* as an interlude within the development or recapitulation, we must locate the beginning of at least one major new section (i.e. the development or recapitulation) prior to it. There is certainly much to recommend the interpretation of Chissell and others, that the development is already in progress before the *Im Legendenton* begins. And the obvious location for the beginning of the development is bar 82, where there is a return to the prevailing tempo after the *Adagio* passage (bar 77); a marked dynamic change from *pianissimo* to *fortissimo*, coupled with a dramatic change of texture and register; a passage of silence articulating bar 82; even the visual clue of a double barline. The apparently new material in bar 82 is in fact truly developmental: the rising contour and syncopated rhythm are surely derived inconspicuously from beats 2–4 of bar 28 in the exposition (Example 4.1). The two passages even share the same initial note. Finally, to hear the wholesale return of the first-group material, first literally at bar 97 and then modified in bar 119, as part of a development section avoids the problem of proposing an exposition spanning bars 1–128 in which the first group appears in the tonic on either side of the second group.

Moreover, there is good reason to understand bar 81 as the end of the second group and of the exposition. The *Adagio* bars 77–81 seem to break up the

Example 4.2: first movement, bars 34–81

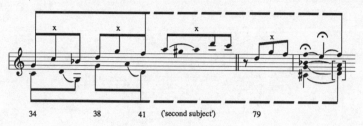

34   38   41   ('second subject')   79

relatively stable situation prevailing since bar 41. More strongly than any other bars in the movement, perhaps, they (and their counterparts, bars 269–73) conjure up the improvisatory rhetorical gestures of the eighteenth-century keyboard fantasy. Instability sets in as early as bar 73, in fact, where the expected cadential F major chord is compromised by the addition of a seventh and the harmony is deflected towards B♭. By bar 81 the previous stable thematic structure has dissolved into recitative, and the harmony is poised on the brink of a cadence in D minor. (Characteristically, Schumann withholds the expected resolution and substitutes D major harmony in bar 83.)

But D minor is the key in which the second group began in bar 41. As Example 4.2 shows, the unrealized cadential chord represented by the solitary, unharmonized f^2 in bar 81 relates back directly to the D minor chord on the downbeat of bar 41.[19] The example also shows that the rising fourth followed by a stepwise descent with which the 'second subject' begins at bar 41 grows directly out of the top voice in the sequential bars 34–41: g^1–c^2–$b♭^1$; d^2–g^2–f^2; a^2–d^3–c^3: the figure is beamed and marked x. Thus the short recitative in bars 79–81 recalls, subtly yet precisely, the introduction of the second group forty bars previously and gives to this section an unsuspectedly unified shape.

What of Daverio's reading, that the recapitulation begins in bar 97 and is interrupted massively by the *Im Legendenton*? The main objection has already been raised by Newcomb: the resulting proportions of the movement (Exposition: 81 bars; Development: 15 bars; Recapitulation, *ex*cluding the 96-bar *Im Legendenton*: 117 bars) are unsatisfactory. Indeed, Daverio himself eventually admits that his reading of the movement against a sonata-form paradigm involves accepting that there is no 'true development'.[20] Even if the (dis)proportions involved in his reading were to seem acceptable, it would be difficult to identify a coherent function for the section formed by bars 82–96.

One further issue remains. Whether we locate the *Im Legendenton* in the

Example 4.3: first movement, bars 1, 128

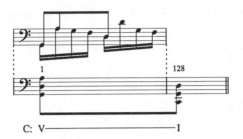

C: V————————————I

development or the recapitulation, we cannot escape the transposed repeat of bars 82–96 in the third section of the movement. That is, Schumann's recapitulation embraces part of the development as well as the whole of the second group. Such a procedure runs counter to conventional sonata-form practice, but was one which Schumann favoured in several movements of his piano sonatas. However much one might criticize the aesthetic effect of these movements, their formal structure is relevant to any sonata-form analysis of the first movement of the *Fantasie*.[21]

Analysis

And yet 'the mistake comes in wanting to claim that the [first movement] is in any *single* form'.[22] More properly, it is mistaken to analyse the movement in terms of a single formal paradigm: its form is *sui generis*. The following analysis discards the problematic sonata-form analogy and invokes no particular formal paradigm for the movement as a whole. It preserves the integrity of the three large sections (bars 1–128; 129–224; 225–309) which no listener is likely to miss and which hark back to the origin of this piece as a single-movement 'fantasy' (see Chapter 2). Thus, the *Im Legendenton* is regarded as a section in its own right rather than as part of some larger formal unit beneath the level of the complete movement.

Section 1 (bars 1–128)

No previous analysis of these bars appears to have recognized the extent to which they form a relatively closed, goal-orientated tonal structure. This is not to deny the ultimate goal, namely the perfect cadence in the tonic at bars 296–7 – the first such cadence in the movement, and the first point of real

Example 4.4: cf. first movement, bars 28–34

c: V⁹   IV⁶₅   V⁸⁻⁷   I

tonal stability. Rather, it is to observe how much that supreme goal and the concomitant tonal grounding of the movement at 'the last possible moment' are prepared in advance.[23]

The movement begins with one and a half bars of the principal accompaniment figure before the right-hand theme (Dahms's *Hauptthema*) is introduced. The accompaniment sets up a dominant pedal which is destined not to resolve definitively until that distant cadence nearly 300 bars later. Beyond the fact that the semiquaver pattern on the first beat anticipates the first three notes (A–G–F) of the theme, it is significant that the figuration projects the underlying vertical combination G–d–a. In bar 128 this is answered by C–G–d, which evokes more than a hint of a V–I cadential progression (Example 4.3). Meanwhile the first internal cadence comes at bars 18–19, where G is barely tonicized before being reinterpreted as V/C once more. The opening material returns, this time in diminished note values, thinner in texture, and with a different continuation.

A second return to the opening music begins with the upbeat to bar 29, but significant changes come into play. The previous pedal harmony is at last quitted: G falls to F, and the opening right-hand a² gives way to a♭². A♭ has already been introduced in an inner voice in bar 28, its effect being to bring the tonic minor region into play. Example 4.4 shows that the chord on the downbeat of bar 29 functions as a subdominant in C minor, suggesting an impending cadence in that key. And this is precisely what occurs: after a passing deflection to E♭ major in bar 33 the bass completes the fifth-descent G–C to usher in a root-position C minor chord on the downbeat of bar 34, concurrently with the arrival of the inner-voice theme which will in due course launch the *Im Legendenton*.[24]

Like the tonicization of G in bar 19, the cadence in C minor proves to be only a temporary resting place, for the music pushes on to the double

Example 4.5: first movement, bars 82–97

sharpward climb through the circle of fifths, first to G and then to D. The arrival of D minor at bar 41 coincides with the putative second subject group already discussed above; no further analysis is necessary here. We should turn instead to bars 82–96, which prepare the fourth appearance of the opening material in bar 97. Bars 82–96 include one of many instances of 'displaced resolution' in the *Fantasie*: that is, they initiate a harmonic progression, the expected goal of which is immediately sidestepped and 'displaced' to a later point. Example 4.5a reveals the underlying voice leading in these bars and shows that a cadence on the dominant of G minor is expected at bar 97. (On this reading the entire passage from bar 82 could be heard as a prolongation of that dominant.) But the harmony in bar 96 does not resolve as expected: the bass moves up from C♯ to D, but the top voice remains on G while the middle voices move up to B and F respectively (Example 4.5b). The result is a dominant seventh in C major and a return to the music from bar 19. The bass D, the fifth of the dominant chord, gives way to its root G at the beginning of bar 98.

Bars 97–105 repeat bars 19–27 almost exactly until the *Im lebhaften Tempo*, beginning on the third beat of bar 105, introduces new material combining a stepwise chromatic bass in syncopated rhythm with an upper voice which seems to emerge from the D–C–B figure heard in bars 102–3 and 104–5. Despite the changed musical surface, the underlying tonal basis remains the same: the harmonic function of this passage is to prolong the dominant seventh

52

Emple 4.6: first movement, bars 117–19

of C, which is clearly stated every two bars between bars 107–13 (the seventh being 'understood' rather than explicitly stated in this last bar). But in bar 113 the main bass note shifts up from G to B♭ and carries with it a harmonic shift from the dominant seventh of C to that of E♭. While the bass pursues its syncopated path downward through two octaves from c♭^{1} to C, the previous quaver movement in the right hand is replaced by a reiterated E♭ dominant seventh. Example 4.6a–c contrasts the actual score of bars 117–19 with two hypothetical versions in order to suggest how unexpected is the actual bar 119, where the bass remains fixed on C while the upper-voice A♭ moves not downward to G (the conventional resolution of this dominant seventh) but upward, spelled now as G♯, to A. Example 4.6b suggests that the return of the opening material in bar 119 might be expected to occur over a continuing dominant pedal in E♭. While this possibility is not realized anywhere in the movement, that shown in Example 4.6c is: the suggestion here is that Section 3 of the movement (bar 225) connects back not only to bar 29 but also, and in a different way, to bar 118.

Bar 119, then, substitutes for a 'displaced' resolution which will not be realized until after the *Im Legendenton*. Nevertheless, the importance of the actual resolution in bar 119 should not be underplayed. On the face of it, bar 119 initiates the fifth appearance of the main thematic material. But in great contrast to all previous appearances, these bars are grounded not on G but on C: the dominant pedal has been replaced by the tonic, although Schumann does not yet offer unalloyed C major harmony. And in terms of texture and dynamics, bar 119 relates more closely to the opening statement (bar 1ff.) than to those at bars 19 and 97.[25] If bars 97–128 are now considered as a larger unit, they appear to correspond formally to a reversal of the two presentations of the main thematic material in bars 1–28, while simultaneously offering a preliminary tonal resolution of that material.

Figure 4.1 summarizes these proposals. Section 1 is analysed as a broadly symmetrical *ABA* form in which the two *A* subsections mirror one another. Bars 29–41, which take the opening material as their starting point, and bars 82–97, which lead back to one form of it, are regarded as transitions. The formal symmetry is not mirrored in the tonal organization, however; as the lowest line of Figure 4.1 shows, the section plays out a V–'I' progression in C ('I' signifying the provisional nature of the tonic arrival at bar 119).[26]

Subsection	A		(trans.)	B	(trans.)	A	
	a1	a2				a2	a1
Bar	1–19	19–28	28–(34)–41	41–81	82–97	97–118	119–28
Tonality	V/C ———————— I/c			d/F/(d)		V/C — 'I'/C	
	V —————————————————————————————— 'I'						

Figure 4.1: First movement, Section 1 (bars 1–128)

To complement Figure 4.1, Example 4.7 presents a voice-leading reduction. This illustrates two hitherto unremarked elements. Firstly, it suggests that a huge expansion of the initial thematic statement in bars 1–10 spans the music up to the return of subsection *A* in bar 97: see the stemmed notes connected by slurs in the top voice. Secondly, it shows how the symmetrical formal structure is supported by certain voice-leading details, notably the two descending fifths G–F–E♭–D–C spanning bars 1–34 and 98–119 (in Example 4.7 these two passages are aligned for easier comparison). The first of these fifths leads to an initial, unstable resolution of the opening dominant pedal on to the tonic minor; the second results in the relatively more stable resolution

Example 4.7: first movement, Section 1 (bars 1–128)

to a provisional form of the tonic major. Allied to these bass progressions is an upper-voice motion involving a^2 and ab^2. In the first case ab^2 replaces the initial a^2 and itself resolves down to g^1 (shown as g^2 in Example 4.7 in order to clarify the expansion of the opening theme; the registral shift from g^1 to g^2 occupies bars 34–9). In the second case the opposite motion occurs: ab^2, functioning as the dominant seventh of Eb, is expected to fall to g^2 but rises instead to a^2, thereby reversing the earlier progression just as the formal sequence *a2–a1* in bars 97–128 reverses that of bars 1–28.

Section 2 (bars 129–224)

We begin not with the *Im Legendenton* itself but with a backward glance at the end of Section 1. The tonic resolution in bars 119–28 has so far been described as 'provisional': this is not yet the pure, unadulterated C major which will break through in bars 296–7 to lead the movement to its close, but rather an amalgam of tonic and dominant chords, expressed most clearly in

55

Emple 4.8: cf. first movement, bars 128–9

the superposition of tonic (C/G) and dominant (G/d) triadic boundaries in the left hand at bar 128. The dominant orientation is strengthened in the *ritardando* passage preceding the double bar. Moreover, the registral limits of this passage – a♭ to G_1 – carefully prepare the tonic minor, as opposed to major, which is to govern the following section.

With such emphatic dominant preparation already provided, why does the *Im Legendenton* insist on a four-bar introduction based upon the dominant *minor*? Why did Schumann not commence as suggested in Example 4.8? In other words, the introduction seems tonally superfluous after bar 128. One possible *raison d'être* for it is perhaps to be found much earlier, at bars 96–7, where the expected cadence on the dominant of G minor was left unrealized (see Example 4.5a). The introductory bars to the *Im Legendenton* partly retrace this earlier passage and supply the resolution displaced at bar 97, establishing thereby a curious link between Sections 1 and 2.

A more palpable link, though one which easily goes unnoticed, is that between the main theme of the *Im Legendenton* and the inner-voice theme in bars 33–7.[27] It is the recurrences of this theme, although no two appearances are identical, which give to the entire section a rondo-like form with a framing introduction and coda (Figure 4.2). Unlike a conventional rondo, none of the *A* subsections is tonally closed, and this makes the coda structurally necessary to the closure of the section as a whole.

	Intro	*A1*	*B*	*A2*	*C*	*A3*	Coda
Bar	129	133	156	173	181	204	216

Figure 4.2

In fact the only statement of the main theme which is closed is the very first one (excluding the introduction), in bars 133–40. What Schumann does here is to allude to the genre of theme and variations: bars 133–40 act like a variation

56

Example 4.9: first movement, bars 152–7 and 206–16

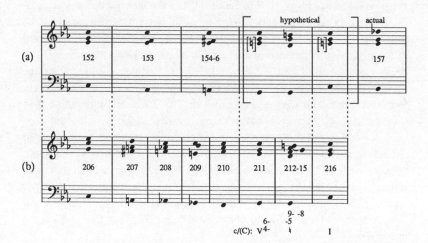

theme, and the following bars present a series of three variations on its first half. The melody is kept more or less intact, the element of variation being contained in the harmonic alternation of C and G minor and the increasingly elaborate accompaniment. The third 'variation', beginning with the upbeat to bar 149, is extended beyond four bars and brings subsection *A1* to a dramatic climax in bar 156. The climax is sidestepped rather than resolved in the following subsection *B*, and to grasp something of the complex meaning of this moment it is necessary to examine the implications of the music rather closely. Example 4.9a shows that the tonal progression set up in bars 152–6 leads the ear to expect a standard cadential resolution in C minor. This resolution comes only much later, in the cadence linking the end of subsection *A3* to the beginning of the coda (see Example 4.9b). These two passages (bars 204–15 and 149–56) are in fact closely connected: they share the same semiquaver figuration, and this yields in each case to cadenza-like writing which leads to a climax. As the chordal reduction in Example 4.9b shows, the later passage is even harmonically similar to the earlier one. There is a sense, in fact, in which subsection *A3* supplies the conclusion to subsection *A1*. It is as if these two main outer subsections of the *Im Legendenton*, temporally separated in performance, are really parts of a single whole.

These considerations only enhance the formal balance and internal coherence of the *Im Legendenton*, characteristics which were held up earlier as quite *un*characteristic of a sonata-form development section. But the *Im Legendenton*

57

does of course draw upon and relate to the music surrounding it: the main theme is taken from bars 33–7 in Section 1, and the introduction supplies the resolution displaced from bars 96–7. Other elements project forward into the music yet to come, the most notable case being the new melodic material heard at the beginning of subsection *B* (bars 156–8 and 158–60). Here Schumann draws upon the allusive music of bars 295–7 (see Chapter 3), but at this stage in the *Im Legendenton* we are ignorant of the significance of what we are hearing. And the forward reference to bars 295–7 is even more subtle than it first seems. The bracketed natural signs before e^1 in the 'hypothetical' bars of Example 4.9a indicate that the implied cadential resolution could occur in the major rather than the minor mode, so that the chord in bars 154–6 would resolve first to a V_4^6 in C major, just as in bars 295–6. The unrealized harmonic implications of bars 154–6 thus point ahead to two different junctures: firstly, to the end of subsection *A3* and the beginning of the coda in the *Im Legendenton*; and secondly, to the crucial bars 295–7 at the end of the movement.[28]

The last two bars of Example 4.9b reveal the harmonic basis of bars 212–16, but it is important not to lose sight (or sound) of the actual musical surface at this point. In particular, the 9–8 suspension is only weakly represented through the grace note g at the end of bar 215. Nor is there a simple C minor triad in bar 216, for ab^2 is tied over from the previous bar. This suspended note harks back to the climactic, prolonged ab^2 at bar 212; and as Example 4.10a shows, the opening of the coda theme is subtly prepared in augmentation by the lead-up to that climax. From this longer-range perspective the true completion of the 9–8 suspension in fact comes not in bar 215 but only with the ab^2–g^2 resolution in bar 217 (Example 4.10b). The resultant emphasis on the step ab^2–g^2 both here and at its repetition in bar 221 helps to link the end of the *Im Legendenton* to the beginning of Section 3, which starts in bar 225 with ab^2–g^2 in the upper voice. The entire range and direction of the coda theme, from ab^2 down to g^1, might even be heard as preparing the first phrase of Section 3, bars 225–9.

Section 3 (bars 225–309)

The opening of this section provides a striking illustration of the way in which context can give quite new meaning to music which is being literally repeated. In this case, bars 225–32 are an exact repetition of the notes of bars 29–36 (the dynamics are slightly altered).[29] But heard now against the firm cadences of the *Im Legendenton*, the C minor implications of the subdominant chord in

Example 4.10

bar 225 are stronger than they were in Section 1, as also is the sense that the immediate tonal goal is not the E♭ cadence in bar 229 but the C minor triad in the following bar. Moreover, if we have hitherto failed to recognize that the main theme of the *Im Legendenton* is derived from the inner voice in bars 33–7, we can hardly miss the connection in bars 229–33. The phrase now cadences on a major rather than a minor triad (compare bars 233 and 37): a change which inevitably calls up our memory of bars 129–32 and suggests that a further function of that anomalous introduction to the *Im Legendenton* is precisely to ensure that the thematic derivation of Section 2 from Section 1 will eventually be heard and understood.

More easily heard and understood is the recapitulation in Section 3 of much of Section 1. But without perfect pitch we are unlikely to perceive the exact level of transposition involved. Rather than hearing a downward transposition from D minor incorporating F major (bars 41–81) to C minor incorporating E♭ major (bars 225–73), we more easily hear a continuation of the tonality of the *Im Legendenton*, the key signature of which is retained until bar 286.[30] It is at this point that the *a2* material from Section 1 (bars 97ff) returns and C minor gives way to C major.[31] The major mode will not be contradicted again. Whereas in Section 1 the return of subsection *a2* led eventually to that of subsection *a1*, here it runs into the allusive *Adagio* section in which, at bar

59

Example 4.11

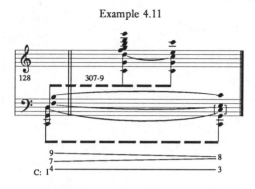

297, Schumann places the first unambiguous root-position tonic triad in the entire movement.

To conclude, we need only consider how the movement as a whole mirrors and magnifies some of the relationships established in Section 1. To work downward from the most global level: the arrival of the tonic in bar 297 and its reiteration thereafter concludes a huge perfect cadence, V–I in C major, within which the entire movement unfolds. Figure 4.1 shows that a similar, smaller-scale cadence offering only a 'provisional' tonic resolution underpins the whole of Section 1. Within that section, two descending fifths, G–C, in the bass lead first to an unstable tonic minor (bars 1–34) and then to a relatively more stable tonic major (bars 1–119). The minor-major conflict has now emerged as a highly-charged element in the tonal organization of the movement, with the tonic minor of the *Im Legendenton* and the first part of Section 3 yielding to the untroubled C major of bars 286–309. Allied to this is the replacement of $a\flat^2$, in the *Im Legendenton* and at bar 225, by a^2 once more at bar 286: here again, the movement as a whole enlarges upon the events of Section 1. Setting the seal on all these connections is the final cadence, during which the tonic–dominant amalgam C–G–D distilled out in the last bar of Section 1 returns in the left hand of bar 307. Formerly unresolved, it dissolves here into the closing triads. Example 4.11 illustrates the point and shows how the repeated final chord provides both the tonal and the registral resolution for bar 128.

5

Schlegel's 'leiser Ton' and thematic unity in the 'Fantasie'

The account of the *Fantasie* in the third (1880) edition of Wasielewski's biography of Schumann differs from that in the first (1858) mainly in its greater dependence on Schumann's own utterances about the work. In particular, Wasielewski quoted Schumann's hint that, in his mind, Clara was the *leiser Ton* of the Schlegel motto (see p. 10). We have seen above that this remark has been burdened with more significance than it was probably intended to bear. Wasielewski, however, even attached a structural significance to the motto, for by 1880 he had come to feel that 'the unifying thread drawing the sequence of ideas together is partly lacking in the [first] movement, and the Schlegel motto was no doubt meant to step in as a support for this'.[1] This is not the place to examine Wasielewski's criticism of the movement, but his words do kindle the issue of the motto and its meaning. If Clara was not really the *leiser Ton*, who or what was? Does the motto point towards some all-embracing unity pervading the *Fantasie*, a unity not immediately evident but rather to be perceived only by 'one who listens in secret'?

Wasielewski took the motto to refer only to the first movement; but in the *Stichvorlage*, where the motto first appears, Schumann had directed that it was to be printed on the verso of the title-page in the first edition. Placed there, it would clearly seem to be a motto for the *Fantasie* as a whole. But Schumann's instructions were not followed, and in the first edition the motto stands at the head of the first movement, which is otherwise untitled. Later editions have all tended to follow suit; one can understand why Wasielewski was misled.

The *Stichvorlage* preserves the most potent evidence that Schumann sought to unify the three movements, for it reveals his plan to repeat the ending of the first movement, from bar 295 onward, at the end of the third. This evidence is also deeply equivocal, since Schumann subsequently suppressed the repeat and substituted the definitive ending played today. We cannot know why he did so; whether, in fact, this was a conscious attempt actually to suppress inter-movement unity, or whether large-scale unification had never

Example 5.1a: first movement, bars 154–7

Example 5.1b: second movement, bars 189–93

Example 5.1c

been an issue anyway. Schumann may simply have come to find the repeat unsatisfactory for other reasons. We might speculate, however, that his decision was based on a mixture of these possibilities. That is, the original ending of the third movement was conceived as a way of unifying the *Fantasie*, but Schumann came to feel that it was too obvious a means to that end. His music, after all, thrives on the subtlety of its musical relationships, and Schumann's love of puzzles and riddles both within music and in other spheres of activity is well known. The unification at the heart of a Schumann work is rarely worn on its sleeve. As an example of this we need look no further in present circumstances than to the transformation of the inner-voice theme in bars 33–7 of the first movement of the *Fantasie* into the main theme of the *Im Legendenton*. Once perceived, the relationship is unmistakable, but it is wont to remain unperceived even after repeated hearing.

The suppressed ending of the third movement, then, might encourage us to seek unity among the three movements of the *Fantasie*, but it should warn us that unifying elements are likely to be less than obvious. Example 5.1 illustrates how seriously that warning should be taken. Example 5.1a shows bars 154–7 of the *Im Legendenton*. As explained in Chapter 4, these bars form the climax of subsection *A1*, a climax which is sidestepped when subsection *B* begins with a reference to the paradoxically yet unheard allusive bars 295–7 at the end of the movement. Example 5.1b shows bars 189–93 of the second movement. These bars also initiate a climactic moment, the final appearance of the main theme. If the two passages are played one after the other, the extraordinary similarity between them sounds through immediately. They both prolong the same diminished-seventh chord, A–C–E♭–G♭/F♯, and they use almost identical notes and textures as a means of doing so. The prolonged bass A eventually resolves up to B♭, and a glance at the chordal reductions of both passages given in Example 5.1c shows how similar is the resolution in the upper voices. The complexity of this inter-movement connection is typical: Schumann refers back to a remote part of the first movement and, far from merely alluding strongly to it, he realizes in the second movement a harmonic implication which was left unstated in the first. It is as if, at bar 189, the second movement merges with, even 'becomes' part of, the first movement. This is repetition of a higher order than that envisaged at the end of the third movement in the *Stichvorlage*. It is intriguing to recall, however, that when he was revising his autograph manuscript of the first movement Schumann considered excising precisely that passage (bars 154–5 and Example 5.1a) to which the second movement alludes most strongly (see Plate 2 and page 16 above).

Unifying factors like this are the exception rather than the norm in the *Fantasie*, however. If we seek Schlegel's 'soft long-drawn note' amid the 'many-coloured dream' of Schumann's music, we do better to investigate the thematic substance of the three movements. Some thematic relationships in

Example 5.2

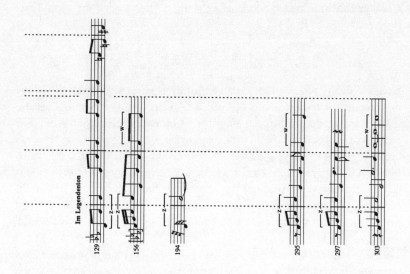

the first movement were considered in Chapter 4, but it is now time to consider them in greater detail before going on to examine the second and third movements also.

The first movement

Example 5.2 presents an analysis of the principal melodic material of the movement: the transpositions of Section 1 in Section 3 are ignored, as also is the transposition of bars 41–50 at bar 61 onward in Section 1 itself. The analysis should be self-evident for the most part, with corresponding elements being aligned vertically to indicate their derivation. The material is divided into two broad groups, labelled I and II, depending on whether the 'parent' comes from the very opening bars – above all, the descending fifth a^2–d^2 in bars 2–6 – or from the cadential figure in bars 14–17. Thus all the melodic material derives from bars 1–19, which Wasielewski termed the 'main idea' (*Hauptgedanke*).

Groups I and II are not mutually exclusive, since certain motivic elements are common to both. For example, the suspension figure *w* is common to the parent statement in group I and to the allusive passage at bar 295, which belongs to group II.[2] Moreover, Example 5.2 accepts a degree of motivic transformation: thus the rising third *z* in II, 14 becomes an octave in I, 28–9 and a rising fourth in I, 41. Indeed, this rising fourth is identified as an element in its own right in II, 194, where d^1–g^1 launches the second part of episode *C* (bars 181–203) of the *Im Legendenton* and is itself transposed up a fourth in bars 198–201. The degree of transformation which these melodic elements can sustain without losing their identity is shown best by the transformation of I, 2 into I, 23, where the descending stepwise contour has been almost totally eradicated and the connection with the parent is maintained largely through the shared rhythmic profile. I, 23 also provides the only instance of an independent motive (here labelled *y*) being generated in a subordinate voice concurrently with a melodic statement in the main voice. The neighbour-note figure a^1–$g\sharp^1$–a^1 embedded in the accompanimental figuration in bar 24 is hardly noticed as a distinct figure at this stage. At its next appearance, in bar 102, the figuration is dispensed with, making motive *y* more obvious. In the meantime, it has provided the beginning of the D minor theme which opens subsection *B* in bar 41: a further example of the typically hidden or 'secret' nature of so many of Schumann's melodic derivations.

Beyond illustrating the number and derivation of melodic elements, Example 5.2 draws attention to an important rhythmic connection between

Example 5.3

the beginning and end of the movement. The parent statement I, 2 undergoes rhythmic diminution at I, 19 and is in fact never heard again in its original rhythmic guise. However, II, 295 and 303 show that the climactic allusive passage undergoes a reverse process, its rhythmic setting being augmented from quavers and crotchets to crotchets and minims. And the relationship between II, 303 and I, 2 is cemented by their almost antecedent–consequent design, whereby the opening dominant-oriented motive *w* is answered by the closing tonic-orientated one (Example 5.3).

Thus the final melodic utterance, II, 303, fuses elements from Groups I and II. Prior to examining the other two movements of the *Fantasie*, we should consider more closely the nature of the thematic process in the first movement. Example 5.2 argues that two particular segments within bars 1–19 generate all the remaining thematic material. This is to conceptualize the process in a conventional way, whereby the seeds of all future development are laid at the outset. But so potent is the arrival of the allusive statement at bar 295 that we may hear this as the single true 'theme' of the movement from which, paradoxically, all previous variants, developments and transformations spring. On this reading the thematic process works in parallel with the tonal one, for it is at bars 295–7 that the first unequivocal statement of the tonic also is presented.

The second movement

The thematic material of this movement discloses a number of close connections with the preceding one. The main theme, which appears at bars 1, 92, and 193, opens with a four-bar phrase (Example 5.4a) whose melodic line proceeds downward by step from scale degree $\hat{5}$ (b♭²), first embellished by an upper neighbour note (c³), to $\hat{2}$ (f²). The neighbour-note motive is labelled

67

Example 5.4a: second movement, bars 1–4

Example 5.4b: first movement, bars 1–19

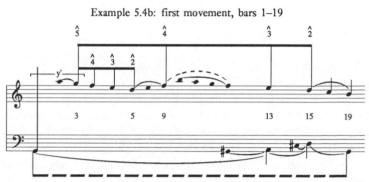

as *y'* to indicate its relationship to the lower neighbour-note motive *y* in Example 5.2. The same basic shape, although unfolded in a much more leisurely fashion, underlies the 'main idea' in bars 1–19 of the first movement, the only real difference being that motive *y'* is incomplete: a^2 is upper neighbour to g^2, which is 'understood' from the opening bass G. In addition, there are two statements of the $\hat{5}$–$\hat{2}$ descent in these bars, one nested inside the other (Example 5.4b). A further connection with the beginning of the first movement emerges in the middle section of the second-movement theme, where the dotted repeated-note figure in bars 9–10 and 13–14 mimics the very opening of the melodic line in the earlier movement.

After the cadence in bars 21–2 a new melodic idea appears in the right-hand inner voice and is taken up imitatively by the lower voices. This idea will itself be subject to variation at later stages (see bars 40ff and 58ff and Example 5.5), but the combination of a rising fourth followed by a stepwise descent proclaims its derivation from I, 41 and I, 79 in Example 5.2 above. What is most conspicuously absent here in the second movement is the lower neighbour-note figure which attaches to the first note of I, 41. This surfaces, however, in the theme of the *Etwas langsamer* section beginning at bar 114.

Example 5.5

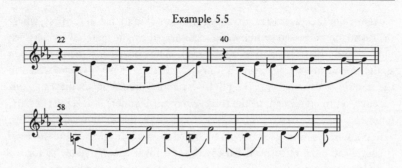

This theme shows a marked affinity with I, 45 in the first movement, as Example 5.6 illustrates.

The third movement

The second movement is straightforward to the extent that the thematic material is presented conventionally. That is, what sounds like the main theme when the movement begins does indeed perform that function and discharges its thematic duty very much as we would expect. It returns at two further points, in its original key and thoroughly recognizable despite the slight variations in its presentation. And its reappearances help us to structure the movement; they give us a sense of knowing where we are.[3] The third

Example 5.6a: second movement, bars 114–18

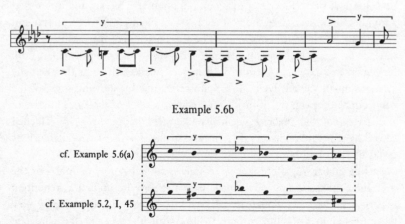

Example 5.6b

movement of the *Fantasie* establishes a situation akin to that in the first, where the distinction between primary and secondary thematic material, or between themes and their derivatives, is blurred. The movement seems to open straightforwardly enough, with a four-bar curtain to a main theme stated in the middle of the texture. The phrase-structure preceding the first obvious cadence, on the dominant of the relative minor (A minor), is 2+(1+1)+2 bars; following the cadence the music starts out from the tonic again with two variations on the initial two-bar phrase heard in bars 5–6. Already the situation is complicated. In retrospect, bars 5–10 seem insufficiently stable to form a complete theme, and it certainly seems too early in the movement for the variational or developmental procedures offered in bars 11–14. We become unsure of where we are. By the end of the movement, when we are so to speak in possession of all the facts, we realize that these opening fourteen bars never return. What initially seemed such a promising theme simply vanishes.

Just as the first movement can be said to be organized around a series of derivatives from the main theme, which itself appears only at bar 295, so the third movement is best understood as building towards a main thematic statement beginning in bar 68. Prior to this a number of thematic elements have been introduced which show a high degree of interrelationship not only with each other but with material from the first movement also. Example 5.7 illustrates and analyses these elements, and shows that the bass of the putative theme in bar 5 is just as 'thematic' as the more conspicuous melody above it.[4]

One important feature of the material in Example 5.7 is the combination of the complete upper neighbour-note figure (y'), first made explicit at the start of the second movement, with the rising fourth (z). Another is the great prevalence of descending stepwise motion, often at a foreground but also at a middleground level (see the beamed notes in Example 5.7; the foreground examples need no special marking). These are prominent features in the first movement, as a glance back at Example 5.2 reveals. And the presence in both movements of extended sections in F major enhances some of the thematic relationships involved. Example 5.8 illustrates this by showing some of the connections between the F-major theme in bars 61–4 of the first movement and several of the thematic elements identified in Example 5.7 (labelled according to bar numbers as 7, 5, 7, 44, and so on).[5] Further such relationships could be found without difficulty.

Starting at bar 72, there is a large-scale modified repeat of much of the preceding music. As already noted, bars 1–14 are omitted; the repetition begins with bar 15. The material heard previously in F major is now recapitulated in C (compare bars 99–122 with 48–71), and the climactic

Example 5.7

Example 5.8

1st movement, bars 61-4

7, 5 (transposed to F)

1, 44

1, 60

(continued on next line)

7, 68

thematic statement beginning at bar 119 is brought to a full close in the tonic (the earlier F major statement had turned inconclusively to the dominant of D minor in bar 71). As a result, the top voice traverses a complete octave, 8̂–1̂, and thus functions appropriately as a *summa* of all previous stepwise descending elements (Example 5.9).

Example 5.9: third movement, bars 119–22

C: I   V   I

The ensuing coda borrows from bars 34–5 before returning to the introductory arpeggiated texture of bars 1–4. Just before the end there emerges from this texture a reference back to the very beginning of the first movement: a^2 is suspended over the barline in bars 134–5 and 136–7 before falling to g^2

Example 5.10a: first movement, bars 2–3

Example 5.10b: third movement, bars 134–5

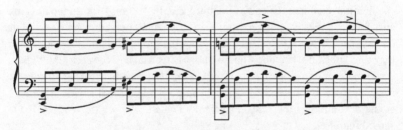

Example 5.10c: first movement, bars 295–7

over the bass G. Example 5.10a–b compares the relevant passages from the first and third movements, and Example 5.10c reveals the relationship of both to the Beethoven/Schubert allusion in bars 295–7 of the first movement, where a¹ functions as upper neighbour to g¹. This same note-pair a¹–g¹ is isolated in the right hand in bar 4 of the third movement, immediately before the apparent exposition of the thematic material gets under way.

Conclusion

There is a high degree of unity in the thematic substance of the three movements of the *Fantasie*. Not that this unity is overtly displayed: the manifold relationships linking thematic elements within and between movements are barely perceptible even in the context of concentrated listening – which is not to say that they are any the less 'real'. And from this vantage point it is perhaps easier to appreciate how Schumann's plan to repeat the end of the first movement at the end of the third may have come to seem too obvious and clumsy a means of advertising the unity which pervades the *Fantasie* in its own special way. Translating back into the terms of Schlegel's motto, we may thus conclude that 'one who listens in secret' can indeed sense a 'soft long-drawn note' amid the 'many-coloured dream'. Yet we still confront an enigma if we try to define this *leiser Ton* more concretely. Is it the thematic statement at the beginning of the first movement? The allusive phrase at its end? Or something else?

In seeking to characterize the thematic process in the *Fantasie* as a whole we may do no better than to borrow from Schumann's critical writings of 1836, the year in which the *Fantasie* was composed. In a review published that August, of several sets of piano variations, Schumann drew attention to the need for 'connection' (*Beziehung*), 'significance' (*Bedeutung*) and 'idea' (*Idee*) in this genre. All three qualities are manifest abundantly in the *Fantasie*. More importantly, discussing the Variations, Op. 15 by Heinrich Elkamp, Schumann described this work as 'a variation-fantasy without a theme . . . a ruin, if you like, for which no critic can establish any rules'.[6] This is a significant description with several interesting ramifications. First, it suggests a highly pertinent way of understanding the thematic process in the *Fantasie*. While we may appreciate the multifarious relationships between the thematic elements, we are at a loss to identify any one statement as the definitive theme from which all other material flows. Looking even to bars 295–7 in the first movement as the thematic kernel, we must confront their equivocal fusion of phrases derived from two different composers, Beethoven and Schubert. Not even here can we find an irreducible thematic component. To conceive of all the thematic material in the *Fantasie* as variations upon an unstated theme is especially appealing, and a powerful way of understanding this profoundly 'secret' work. In addition, there is the fact that in January 1839 Schumann told Clara that he had completed a work called *Guirlande* which consisted of 'variations but with no theme'; Elkamp's Op. 15 evidently lingered in Schumann's memory (see p. 74).[7] Finally, there is Schumann's suggested description of the Elkamp variations as a 'ruin', a word which he also used as the title for the first movement of the *Fantasie*. Schumann's use of the same word, *Ruinen*, to describe Chopin's *Preludes*, Op. 28 is better known than the Elkamp reference. On the other hand, the Elkamp review is chronologically much closer to the *Fantasie*; and we should not let the obscurity into which the work and its composer have fallen interfere with its implications for a better understanding of Schumann's *leiser Ton*.

6

Form in the second and third movements

The attention traditionally accorded the first movement of the *Fantasie* has resulted in the second and third movements being decidedly neglected. Chapter 5 has begun to redress the balance by considering aspects of the thematic process in these movements and the relationship of their thematic material to that of the first movement. The purpose of this chapter is to examine their formal structures, for each is in its own way as original and problematic as the first movement.

The second movement

This movement has been the least discussed of the three. Wasielewski regarded it basically as a rondo form; Dahms thought it a 'marchlike rondo' whose formal structure was plain to see (*übersichtlich*); for Chissell it is 'a sonata-rondo, an easy solution to the problem of large-scale architecture'; even Linda Correll Roesner, whose analyses of the first and third movements of the *Fantasie* stress the originality of Schumann's approach to form, regards it as 'relatively straightforward in structure'.[1] The rondo analogy arises obviously enough from the unmistakable entries of the opening theme; the sonata-rondo qualification tries to account for the transposed 'recapitulation' of a substantial secondary passage. Indeed, it is precisely because a background paradigm *seems* so much more obvious and unequivocal here that the second movement has been so consistently ignored. But rondo is not the formal paradigm against which this movement plays, and closer examination reveals an unsuspected formal complexity.

In Figure 6.1 the movement is analysed in terms of a large *ABA* or da capo structure, March I–Trio–March II. The formal paradigm also assumes an internal *ABA* structure for the March and Trio individually. March I initially inspires confidence that this movement of the *Fantasie*, at least, *will* be straightforward. The opening section *A* establishes a four-bar phrase norm, and the tonal and cadential structure is transparently clear. When the dynamic

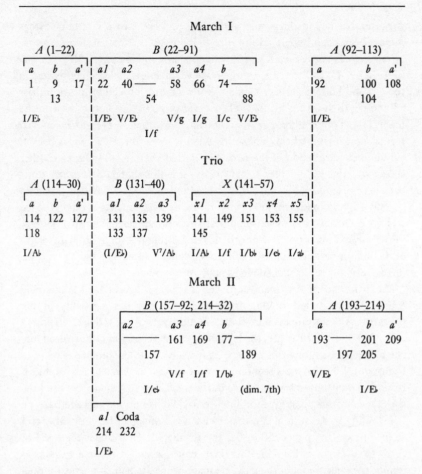

Figure 6.1: second movement

level drops at bar 22 and new rhythmic and melodic ideas emerge, there is little doubt that we have entered the middle section of a three-part form which will be completed – sooner rather than later – by the repetition, perhaps with a few modifications, of section *A*. The first doubts arise with bar 40. After the brief tonal digression around bar 33, the return to a *forte* dynamic (bar 35) and a dominant seventh of E♭ (bar 39) seem to announce the impending return of *A* at bar 40. Instead, the dominant harmony is retained and there is a return to the situation at bar 22.

The continuation brings some reassurance. The low dominant pedal suggests that our instincts were right, and that the return of section *A* has merely been slightly delayed in order to increase its eventual impact: a case of *reculer pour mieux sauter*. But new doubts arise when the low B♭ gives way to A♭ in bar 45, and they can but increase when a new melodic idea enters in the top and bottom parts of bars 50–4. Two more subsections begin in bars 58 and 66, each taking bar 22 as their point of departure but set now in the tonal context of G minor. Far from returning to section *A*, events have moved a good deal further afield. This impression is strengthened when, at bar 74, yet another incarnation of the pervasive dotted rhythm inaugurates another subsection, one *not* indebted to bar 22. But it is this subsection *b* which leads back to the dominant seventh of E♭ at bar 88 and thence to the return of section *A*, only slightly modified, in bars 92–113. The final cadence is strengthened by a $^{6-5}_{4-3}$ extension, and the ensuing beat's rest reinforces the sense of closure in this large *ABA* form. The only disturbing element – the inordinate length of the middle section compared to the outer ones – recedes as the Trio begins in the relaxing key of the subdominant, A♭.

The Trio, too, at first seems a model of its kind, except for the lingering echoes of the dotted rhythm from March I. But the normality of the proceedings again proves short-lived when the return of section *A*, expected at bar 141 (compare bar 118, the beginning of the repetition of the basic four-bar phrase constituting this section), is replaced by the section labelled *X* in Figure 6.1. This balances section *A* almost exactly in terms of length, but it really has no counterpart elsewhere in the movement, let alone the Trio: the *scherzando* marking is as much an intellectual joke as a performance indication.

Beginning in A♭, section *X* works round to F minor in bar 149, whence a series of two-bar sequences pushes the tonality down through the cycle of fifths to A♭ minor at bar 155. The final sequence steps back one stage to E♭ minor, the tonic minor of the movement as a whole, to launch the next formal surprise. With no warning whatsoever bar 157 catapults us back into the March, although at a point well past its beginning. Bars 157–88 correspond almost exactly to bars 54–87 of March I: the March II version is slightly extended and the harmonic goal is different (compare bars 88 and 189). The four-bar preparation beginning at bar 189 balances in length that in bars 88–91; it is also the passage which relates back to bars 154–6 of the first movement (see Chapter 5).[2]

What happens at bar 157 makes us re-evaluate bar 54. This hardly seemed a strong point of articulation in March I, but it takes on new significance when it becomes the point at which the fragmentary March II begins. Schumann's final surprise, however, is to make us reconsider perhaps our earliest and most fundamental assumption about the movement: the identity of section A in the March. Bar 193 marks the beginning of the third section of March II, the first section A having been entirely omitted. (The setting of bars 193–6 over an $E\flat^6_4$ rather than the previous root-position triad may be intended as a sign of their formal position.) Bar 214 should therefore bring the return of bar 113, the closing bar of March I. But bar 214 corresponds to bar 22, and rather than coming to a definite stop the movement continues with the first subsection ($a1$) of section B from March I. The whole of the subsection is repeated at pitch, the only change coming in the final bars when the retention of the dominant triad in March I (see bars 39–40) is replaced by a perfect cadence establishing the tonic for the beginning of the coda in bar 232.

Bars 214–32 have three functions. First, they supply (untransposed) the subsection missing from the transposed repetition of section B of March I which begins at bar 157.[3] Secondly, in ending with a perfect cadence which then launches a new section – the coda – they confirm the original supposition that section B of March I would end at bar 40, rather than continuing until bar 91. Thirdly and most importantly, we now hear bars 193–232 as a single, closed unit. And this makes us wonder, now almost at the end of the movement, whether section A of March I really does consist only of bars 1–22 or whether in fact it extends to bar 40, with all the implications for the rest of our analysis that this reinterpretation would entail. It is because the second movement of the *Fantasie* continually brings us up short in our assumptions about what is happening or is about to happen – because it repeatedly seems to tell us one thing while meaning another – that it is every bit as challenging and original as the two movements which surround it, to say nothing of the technical demands it makes upon every performer.

The third movement

Commentators perplexed by the form of this movement have tended to avoid the risk of attaching analytical labels, taking refuge instead in descriptions of their emotional response to it. For Dahms it was 'pure poetry'; for Solomon, 'the finale is unorthodox' but brings 'spiritual calm after the upheaval of the preceding drama'; Chissell hears 'a deep, introspective meditation'. Wasielewski, on the other hand, assigned it to *Liedform*, with two main themes (*Hauptsätze*) in C and A♭ which are characteristically combined in a coda. And Dale referred to 'an extended dual form new to Schumann'. While she declined to give a closer analysis of the term, it is difficult not to see in it a harbinger of Roesner's 'parallel' form.[4]

Perhaps the most original formal feature of the movement is one already touched upon in Chapter 5. Bars 1–14 are entirely omitted from the large-scale transposed repetition which begins in bar 72. A pivotal consequence of their omission is that the apparent main theme which begins in bar 5 after a four-bar introduction is recognized retrospectively as no such thing: the opening of the movement behaves rather like a mirage, the *fata morgana* which had so entranced Schumann early in 1838. The first really firm thematic statement is delayed until bar 68, by which time the tonality has shifted to the subdominant, F major.

The jettisoning of the opening section in the context of a large-scale repeat, and the process whereby a stable theme evolves from a series of subtly related derivatives, are two respects in which the third movement of the *Fantasie* mimics the first. Others could be cited, such as the use of the subdominant as a secondary key area or the use of third-related keys within formal sections (D minor/F major in the first movement, A♭ major/F major in the third). In other respects, however, the two movements differ sharply. However unsatisfactory the sonata-form paradigm may be in relation to the first movement, its terminology simply cannot responsibly be applied to the third. Ironically enough, the third movement does fulfil one of the cardinal conditions of sonata form eschewed by the first: the repetition in C major of the thematic material first heard in F provides the large-scale dissonance-resolution characteristic of the recapitulation of sonata-form second groups (see Chapter 4). By contrast, the 'second-group' material heard in D minor/ F major in the 'exposition' of the first movement is 'recapitulated' in C minor/ E♭ major. Another difference is to be found in overall tonal strategies. While the first movement may be conceptualized as a hugely protracted perfect cadence in C, the first tonic affirmation being delayed almost until the end, the third movement does not obscure the tonic at the outset. There is movement in two directions here, away from and back to the tonic key. The tonal motion in the first movement, meanwhile, is essentially uni-directional.[5]

Figure 6.2 provides a synopsis. The 'dual' or 'parallel' form is clarified in the alignment of the corresponding bars of the two main sections. Taken at face value, the movement could be read as a fairly straightforward *A1 A2 B || A2 B* + coda structure. As in the second movement, however, our perception of the succession of events is subject to modification as each new piece of evidence accrues. Thus *A1 A2* in Section I may come to seem like a long introductory passage standing outside the main movement. Bars 30–3 clearly have the same introductory function, and even the same texture, as bars 1–4: perhaps, then, the movement proper begins here, or even with the

80

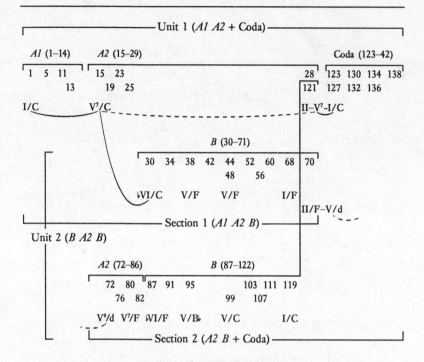

Figure 6.2: third movement

Etwas bewegter at bar 34. But this hypothesis is spoilt by the return of *A2* in bars 72–86, and thus we return to the more straightforward two-section view outlined in Figure 6.2.

But things are less straightforward than Figure 6.2 suggests. We need to reconsider the beginning of Section II, which is not as definitive as it seems on a casual reading of the score. The thematic statement beginning at bar 68 appears set to close in that key: we expect a II–V⁷–I cadence in F at bar 71. But the tonality is deflected away from F major to D minor and Section I closes with an imperfect cadence, IV–V, in that key.[6] It is on this dominant harmony – note the retained low A in the left hand – that Section II begins with its transposed repetition of *A2*. Despite all the visual evidence of a pause sign and double bar, the harmonic continuity from bars 71–2 (emphasized in Figure 6.2 by the broken slur linking the harmonic symbols V/d and V⁹/d) complicates the two-section analysis. Paradoxically, it strengthens the relationship between the two *A2* subsections. The first, beginning at bar 15, is understood as following on directly from the harmony reached at the end

Example 6.1

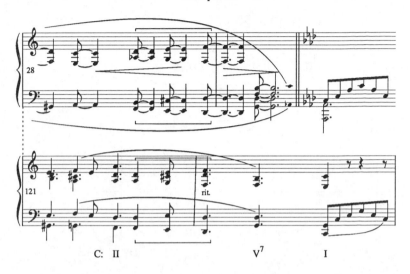

C: II   V⁷   I

of bar 14: the bass falls a fifth from D to G while ff³ in the top voice falls to f³. The retained harmony between bars 71–2 prepares the second subsection *A2* in a similarly seamless way, and even suggests that the bars preceding bar 72 function somehow as a substitute for the missing bars 1–14, while being quite unlike them in any obvious sense.

In a sense, it is the expected II–V⁷–I cadence in F at bar 71 which provides the key to the whole structure. When the corresponding point is reached at bar 122 in Section II the cadence is duly forthcoming, although now in C rather than F major. But bars 121–2 reach back well beyond bar 71, to bars 28–9. Here also a II–V⁷–I cadence in the tonic was prepared, only to be sidestepped by the surprise resolution to the flattened submediant, A♭, in bar 30. The harmony of bars 121–2 duplicates the earlier cadential preparation almost exactly (Example 6.1) and supplies its withheld tonic resolution at the beginning of the coda. The unbroken slurs incorporated into Figure 6.2 are intended to highlight the large-scale harmonic progressions between bars 1, 15, and 30 as well as the structural cadence in bars 121–2. The broken slurs suggest the large-scale retention of the unresolved dominant seventh in C between bars 15–29 and 29–122.

Dale's notion of a 'dual' form proves particularly apt for this movement, although her sense of 'dualism' may not have been that understood here. Figure 6.2 tries to suggest that the configuration of the various subsections

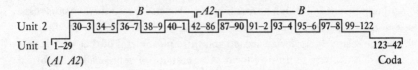

Figure 6.3: third movement (cf. Figure 6.2)

is better understood in terms of two units, *A1 A2* coda (Unit 1) + *B A2 B* (Unit 2). Unit 2, in which all the main motion away from the tonic takes place, is embedded within Unit 1, whose essentially connected and tonally closed structure is severed following bar 29. Still another way to conceptualize the form of the movement is to borrow a spatial metaphor and to imagine that Unit 1 is not so much severed as submerged by Unit 2. This interpretation gives new meaning to bars 30–3, 36–7, 40–1 and 87–90, 93–4, 97–8. According to Figure 6.2 these bars belong to the two *B* subsections and thus to Unit 2. But above all they evoke bars 1–4, which belong to Unit 1. These short passages create the impression that Unit 1 continues as it were 'beneath' Unit 2, largely unheard but occasionally breaking through to the aural surface. Figure 6.3 attempts to illustrate something of this layered understanding of the movement. Bars 30–3, 36–7, 40–1, 87–90, 93–4 and 97–8 are horizontally aligned as constituents of Unit 2, just as in Figure 6.2; but they are also bracketed and highlighted by bold print in order to suggest that fundamentally they represent the continuing presence of Unit 1, which spans the entire movement.

One further ramification of this view awaits consideration. Wasielewski wrote of the two main themes in C and A♭ which are 'characteristically combined' (*eigenthümlich gemischt*) in the coda. In reality, the *Etwas bewegter* melody from bars 34–5 is heard in C major above an accompaniment which derives from bars 1–4. These four bars cannot fail to be heard immediately as introductory to the theme beginning in bar 5: the theme which turns out to have been but a mirage. Figure 6.3 offers the possibility that the quaver accompaniment in bars 1–4, far from being merely introductory, is itself the primary *thematic* element in the tonic key; it is precisely this accompaniment which repeatedly breaks the surface following bar 29 and which is celebrated in the coda, where the long-awaited continuation and resolution of bar 29 at last takes place. 'You know nothing of my larger compositions, sonatas . . . here, I think (if not already in the smaller works), you would see how many and what new forms they contain.'[7] Schumann wrote thus to his friend the composer Herrmann Hirschbach on 7 September 1838, when the *Fantasie* was still unpublished. Though he mentions only sonatas specifically, he must have counted the *Fantasie* among his 'larger' compositions. Not only the first but also the relatively neglected second and third movements of this work reflect his rare sensitivity to musical form. All questions of genre aside, the formal richness of the *Fantasie* is indeed *durchaus phantastisch*.

7

The subsequent history of the 'Fantasie'

Critical reception

'I know my path is a fairly lonely one, with no large crowd cheering along the way to spur [me] on to work. Besides, I am understood only by a few, but for that I am compensated by three people's love: Liszt's, Clara Wieck's – and now yours.'[1] This passage from a letter Schumann wrote to his Belgian admirer Simonin de Sire on 8 February 1838 aptly sums up his public profile during the 1830s. His music was not widely appreciated: it was too intellectually demanding and eschewed the easy virtuosity characteristic of so many compositions of the period.[2] Thus he was delighted by de Sire's opinion that 'R. Schumann is *primus inter omnes*!', and by his request for copies of Schumann's complete piano works. On 15 March 1839 Schumann again wrote to de Sire, listing all his published works to date. He mentioned the *Fantasie*, which 'has just appeared at Breitkopf's', and there can be no doubt that de Sire would have procured a copy as soon as possible.[3]

Liszt's response to the *Fantasie*, dedicated to him by Schumann, is considered below in connection with its performance history, and something of Clara's excitement on receiving and learning the new work was noted in Chapter 1. Clara's response is obviously fundamental to any sketch of the reception of the *Fantasie*; her particular favourite seems to have been the second movement, and on 16 June 1839 she wrote from Paris outlining her personal 'programme' for it to Schumann: 'The march strikes me as a victory march of warriors returning from battle, and in the A♭ section I think of the young girls from the village, all dressed in white, each with a garland in her hand crowning the warriors kneeling before them.' Predictably, perhaps, she confessed further that she imagined herself as one of the white-clad maidens, welcoming home and crowning Robert her beloved warrior and conqueror.[4]

Among other intimates of Schumann who appreciated his music was his former teacher Heinrich Dorn. Dorn had got to know the *Fantasie* by 19 June 1839, when he wrote to Schumann from Riga saying that 'your recent Liszt-sonata gave me great pleasure; in the first movement I would have liked one or two *Latin* passages (as Probst says) Germanized. The rest is excellent.'[5] But it was not until some five years later that what seems to have been the first printed criticism of the *Fantasie* appeared. The composer Carl Kossmaly offered to write a review of Schumann's piano music for the Leipzig music paper, the *AMZ*. Schumann sent him a parcel of some of his 'older' works together with a covering letter on 5 May 1843 explaining that these pieces were all little known for obvious reasons: because of their difficult form and content; because Schumann himself had been unable to perform them in public; because, as editor of the *NZfM*, he could not be seen to be advertising his own music; and because Gottfried Fink, editor of the rival *AMZ*, was hostile to it and would therefore not give it any publicity. Now, he continued, things had quite changed; the public was more sympathetic to his work, and even to the earlier pieces.[6]

Schumann's letter is itself an important document for a reception history of his music. As for Kossmaly, he wrote a lengthy essay called 'On Robert Schumann's Piano Compositions' which appeared in three instalments in the *AMZ* for January 1844.[7] While its early date makes it a particularly valuable piece of criticism, it is unfortunate (if inevitable) that Kossmaly contented himself mostly with vague generalizations about Schumann's style rather than dealing in any depth with individual works. The quotations which follow are taken from the abridged translation of the article which appeared in the American *Dwight's Journal of Music* after Schumann's death. *Dwight's Journal* gave considerable space to Schumann's music and is a useful gauge of his transatlantic reputation.[8]

Kossmaly began by lamenting the obsession with excessive technical display at the expense of true artistic worth which, in his view, had characterized piano music during the preceding years. He found it natural, however, that original artistic creation should take longer to be accepted by the public, and prophesied that Schumann's music, which of course belonged in this category, would one day be accorded its proper recognition. Although highly supportive of Schumann, Kossmaly was not wholly uncritical:

In all the piano compositions of Schumann one remarks a constant striving after peculiarity, after originality in form and matter . . .

This . . . sometimes disturbs us greatly; the wish to be always new and striking, and always produce something extraordinary, is too clearly prominent. Still more does it put us out of tune when this striving degenerates at times into a mere search for strange, unheard of turns and effects, into utterly unenjoyable *bizzarrerie*.

Kossmaly traced this *bizzarrerie* to Schumann's sympathy with the 'New Romanticism', of which originality, obscurity and intellectuality were articles of faith. As examples of early works exhibiting these 'new Romantic' tendencies he chose the *Allegro*, Op. 8, the *Etudes symphoniques*, Op. 13, the *Concert sans orchestre*, Op. 14, the F♯ minor Sonata, Op. 11 (but called Op. 15 by Kossmaly), and the *Fantasie*, Op. 17. Of the *Fantasie* he wrote that it unquestionably

affords the richest and yet most unquickening luxuriance of this neo-Romantic *hypergeniality*. The eccentric, the arbitrary, the vague and undetermined, could scarcely be pushed farther. The transcendentalism, so loved before all things, degenerates at times here into madness and utter unintelligibleness, while the striving after originality loses itself in the unnatural and overstrained. The composer reminds us of a rich nobleman, who, to make himself inaccessible to all approach in his aristocratic superiority, selfishly fences himself in from the world . . . and so fortifies and palisades himself that people are discouraged from seeking nearer acquaintance with him.

As welcome exceptions to these criticisms, Kossmaly cited *Carnaval* and the *Davidsbündlertänze*. Then proceeding chronologically through Schumann's works, he identified a gradual process of simplification and a gain in independence. *Kinderszenen* seemed to him a highly successful piece in this more accessible style, but 'the gems of the whole collection' were the *Humoreske* and the Sonata in G minor. In view of the more recent tendency, discussed below, to regard the *Fantasie* as a 'surrogate sonata' with which Schumann's published sonatas compare unfavourably, Kossmaly's evidently greater sympathy with the G minor sonata is striking. As for the 'madness and utter unintelligibleness' of the music, a similar initial response to the *Fantasie* was claimed by the critic Ker (the pseudonym of Christian Louis Heinrich Köhler) in an article published in *SmW* in 1849.[9]

The four editions of Wasielewski's pioneering biography, published between 1858 and 1906, form an important link between the nineteenth and twentieth centuries. Wasielewski was never in any doubt that the *Fantasie* was one of Schumann's most significant compositions prior to 1840, even if by 1880, when the third edition of his book appeared, he sensed a certain lack of unity in the first movement (see Chapter 5). His aesthetic judgement of the *Fantasie* otherwise remained essentially unchanged. A peculiarity of Wasielewski's original (1858) account is the claim that the three movements of the 'Sonata for Beethoven' were to be called 'Ruins' (*Ruinen*), 'Triumphal Arch' (*Triumphbogen*), and 'Starry Crown' (*Sternenkranz*).[10] The evidence, if any, for this last name remains obscure, but it has been adopted in several later texts both in English and German.

One such was the first edition (1903) of Abert's book on Schumann, which also went through several editions up to the early 1920s. As noted in Chapter

Example 7.1: first movement, bars 77–81, as texted by Friedrich von Hausegger

3, Abert seems to have been the first commentator to suggest a relationship between Schumann's first movement and Beethoven's *An die ferne Geliebte*. The announcement came in the second edition, published in 1910, where Abert also suggested that the triumphal character of the second movement was influenced by Weber's *Euryanthe* although he identified no specific part of the opera to substantiate his case.[11] Abert's 1910 account of the *Fantasie* is less concerned with matters of compositional technique than that of 1903. Here Abert identified bars 65–8 of the first movement (Schumann's 'favourite passage', as he told Clara) as the melodic source of everything else and claimed that this was the first piece in which Schumann attempted to build a whole movement from a single motive. And to the extent that the theme always remains a closed whole, development being achieved by means of the juxtaposition and transposition of sharply defined musical periods, Abert claimed a relationship with Schumann's symphonic technique. Discussion of Schumann's developmental methods brought a comparison with Beethoven: for Abert, Schumann's tendency to build large forms from small motives meant that Beethoven's long drawn-out (*langathmig*) and profound (*tiefsinnig*) melodic combinations were unavailable to him. Development accordingly became a process of placing one thing *next to* another rather than deriving one thing *from* another.[12] This unfavourable comparison with Beethoven's handling of large-scale form has become standard both in German and English critical writing on Schumann and sonata form.[13] Nonetheless, in terms of its conceptual content (*Gedankeninhalt*), by which he meant basically the translation into music of Schumann's temporarily thwarted love for Clara, Abert considered the *Fantasie* to be closer to Beethoven than any of Schumann's other early works.[14] And Walter Dahms evoked Beethoven in his book on Schumann, specifically drawing a parallel between the unusual three-

Example 7.2: first movement, bars 116–20, as texted by Giovanni Menotti

Lud -wig! Ludwig! Lud -wig! Lud-wig! unser Lud - wig van Beet- ho - ven!

movement form of the *Fantasie* and Beethoven's own Op. 27 'fantasy-sonatas'.[15]

It is inevitable that assessment of the *Fantasie* should have been influenced, always favourably, by awareness of the *grande passion* which largely inspired it. The eagerness of critics to read Schumann's life into the music could be said to have inspired a tradition of hermeneutic analysis in both German and English writing. Even Abert fits in here, in that his *An die ferne Geliebte* allusion may be construed as a means by which Schumann sends a message to Clara using Beethoven and his poet Alois Jeitteles as intermediaries. For a more enthusiastic reading of this kind, however, we must turn to Friedrich von Hausegger, who in 1903 proposed that the first movement of the *Fantasie* 'speaks' to Clara in very specific terms: thus, the *Adagio* passage at bar 77 presents the 'faltering question': 'Are you then truly lost to me?', followed by the outburst 'Farewell, my beloved' (Example 7.1).[16]

Whereas for Hausegger it was Clara's presence (or absence) which hung heavy over the first movement, Giovanni Menotti went much further than Abert or anyone else in reading the work as a tribute to Beethoven. For Menotti, the allusions to Beethoven's music spread far beyond the song cycle to embrace the 'Eroica' Symphony, the Piano Sonatas, Op. 31 and 81a, and even the Ninth Symphony. And Menotti's derivation of a kind of *Uridee* from selected musical letters in the name Ludwig van Beethoven makes the riddle of the Sphinxes in *Carnaval* utterly unmysterious by comparison. Since the specificity of Menotti's obsessive reading demands concrete illustration, Example 7.2 presents part of the 'hymn of praise' in which the voices of Florestan and Eusebius 'break out in frenetic rapture'.[17]

A common element in English commentaries on the first movement of the *Fantasie* is the identification of the falling five-note figure at the very opening as 'Clara's theme'. This particular tradition goes back to Robert Schauffler's

1945 book on Schumann which suggested that the three piano sonatas and the *Fantasie* are interlinked by their use of the 'single germ- and source-motive' C–B♭–A♭–G–F, derived from a work by Clara which Schauffler nonetheless does not identify.[18] Building upon Schauffler's approach, the work of Eric Sams in the 1960s proposed a far more sophisticated system of musical ciphers according to which Clara's name and other words are literally encoded in Schumann's music.[19]

In the main, however, English criticism has been content with a fairly consistent view of Schumann as a successful miniaturist who was less able to write convincingly for the piano on a larger scale. Thus the three sonatas are generally regarded as flawed works while the *Fantasie* (above all, its first movement) is viewed as a shining exception, a surrogate sonata in which the power of Schumann's inspiration enabled him to overcome his problems with large-scale form.[20] In 1905 Edward Dannreuther could write that 'the fantastic miniatures that go to make up . . . some numbers of the Phantasie in C and *Kreisleriana* . . . are each the brief expression of a single mood, each remarkable for concentration and power of suggestion. But this method of stringing together a number of independent paragraphs . . . does not commend itself.' The view of the *Fantasie* as a work consisting of 'numbers', some of them constructed from independent miniatures, is intriguing; presumably Dannreuther was thinking mainly of the first movement. But he went on to suggest that apart from the Piano Concerto, 'none of Schumann's larger pianoforte works [Opp. 11, 13, 14, 17, 20, 21, 22] are entirely without flaw or shortcoming . . . the formative power is defective or imperfectly developed; the materials are not completely welded together . . . the music is not so much an organic whole as it is a fusion of parts.'[21]

Much the same attitude is taken in Kathleen Dale's lengthy and useful discussion of the piano music in the *Symposium* edited by Gerald Abraham and published in 1952: '[Schumann's] gifts were not those of a clear-sighted architect, and his sonatas consequently convey little sensation of being compact structures whose ground-plan was determined from the very beginning. Yet though his long-range architectonic planning was deficient, his artistic power of filling large spaces with enchanting musical images was highly developed.'[22] And the idea that fine wine may be contained within an imperfectly shaped bottle can also be found in Joan Chissell's assessment of the sonatas. For Chissell, however, writing in 1972, the emotional and autobiographical well-springs of the *Fantasie* enabled Schumann to overcome 'all those formal problems that had dogged him before in larger canvases. Though headed "Fantastic and passionate throughout" . . . the first movement is nevertheless the most masterly of all his keyboard arguments in sonata form. The ideas, all vintage Schumann, merge into each other without visible seams, as do the larger sections.' And the third movement comes as 'a profound benediction. Nothing in the earlier sonatas, or indeed any of his previous works, springs from such deep places of the heart.'[23]

Implicit in all these discussions is the belief that it is legitimate to evaluate Schumann's sonatas against the Classical model derived from Haydn, Mozart, and Beethoven. One of the more positive assessments is that of Yonty Solomon, for whom 'Schumann's three sonatas, and the C major Fantasie, represent an intriguing phenomenon . . . [gathering] together the first positive threads towards recreating and reassessing the dominant form of the Classical era.' For Solomon, 'it is far from the truth to believe that Schumann's themes are not capable of development by motivic elaboration. They are often so developed, their rich potential worked out, before the Development section proper gets under way.'[24] And yet it is Solomon's account of the first movement of the *Fantasie*, already cited in Chapter 4, which most unquestioningly applies the conventional terminology of sonata form to the music.

Other writers, including several American musicologists, have been at pains to avoid the all-too-easy equation with sonata form. Charles Rosen began the Epilogue of his *The Classical Style* with the claim that 'Robert Schumann's homage to Beethoven, the Fantasy in C major, Op. 17, is the monument that commemorates the death of the classical style.' Far from having anything to do with the Classical sonata, Rosen hears in the music of the first two movements 'a return to the principles of the Baroque'.[25] The recently popular tendency to apply to music concepts derived from literary theory has made its mark on Schumann's music, not least the *Fantasie* itself. John Daverio's analysis of the first movement, discussed in Chapter 4, takes as its starting point Schlegel's concept of the *Arabeske*. Daverio's approach had been anticipated some years earlier, however, by Gernot Gruber, who explored the interpretative potential of Schlegel's literary forms and theories, and particularly his concept of the *Arabeske*, in relation to the movement.[26] Anthony Newcomb's exploration of 'narrative strategies', while its understanding of 'narrative' has been challenged, offers a reading of a musical score against a 'paradigmatic plot' which is the model for the analysis of the second movement of the *Fantasie* in Chapter 6. Finally, Linda Correll Roesner's treatment of Schumann's 'parallel' forms argues that in his sonatas Schumann used ' "traditional" gestures . . . as diversions deliberately to obscure what is really happening'; the *Fantasie* and *Concert sans orchestre* in particular exemplify his 'total rethinking of sonata structure'.[27]

Editions

The first edition of the *Fantasie*, bearing the plate number 6053, was published by Breitkopf & Härtel in March or April 1839. In 1841 an edition with a revised title-page (*Titelauflage*) appeared, the revision being occasioned by the need to alter the price in line with the currency reform which took place in Saxony in that year. Lest this be thought to indicate that the edition was selling well, it should be noted that later impressions (*Abzüge*) of the first edition, bearing the original price, were still retailing in the early 1860s.[28] Two important later editions stem from Clara: the one included in the collected edition of Schumann's works published between 1879–93 and in the preparation of which Brahms played a major role; and Clara's 'instructive edition' (*Instructive Ausgabe*) of the piano works, published in 1887. The first impression of this edition is notable for Clara's deletion of the dedication to Liszt, although it was subsequently restored.[29]

The growth in popularity of Schumann's piano music in the later nineteenth century is reflected in the number of editions prepared by celebrated pianists. Two examples are those of Ernst Pauer and Agnes Zimmerman, both of which first appeared in the 1880s. Pauer and Zimmerman lived and worked in England though neither was English by birth. Zimmerman's Schumann edition is notable for having been one of the first English publications to use the 'continental' fingering system. That the *Fantasie* had become popular at an earlier date is suggested by the fact that Breitkopf & Härtel published a four-hand version in 1867.[30] The most authoritative modern edition to date is that edited by the veteran Schumann scholar Wolfgang Boetticher with a preface dated 'Göttingen, Frühjahr 1987' and published by Henle. This edition prints the deleted ending of the third movement preserved in the *Stichvorlage* and curiously gives '1835/1836' as the date of composition, although there is no evidence to support the earlier year. With the recently inaugurated *Neue Ausgabe sämtlicher Werke Robert Schumanns* (*RSA*) now under way, a new scholarly edition of the *Fantasie* may be expected in the future.

Performance history

Schumann's letter to de Sire quoted above links the two nineteenth-century keyboard giants with whom the *Fantasie* is closely associated: Clara Wieck, indisputably the 'subject' of the first movement, and Franz Liszt, to whom the work was dedicated. Both responded very positively to the publication of the *Fantasie* while being equally positive that it was unlikely to receive an immediately favourable reception from the public. Schumann was not backward in advising Clara as to which of his works she might successfully perform on her concert tours, and despite her raptures over the *Fantasie*, there is no suggestion in their letters to one another in the second half of 1839 that it would be a suitable choice.[31]

Schumann had written to Liszt on 14 January 1839 telling him of his intention to dedicate the *Fantasie* to him, and perhaps expressing his misgivings about its potential in the concert hall. Liszt replied on 1 March, telling of the great esteem and sympathy in which he had always held his 'colleagues' Chopin and Schumann: 'you will therefore easily understand . . . what a pleasure it is for me to accept the piece which you intend for me! However unsuitable it may be for public performance, do not doubt at all that I shall do everything in my power to give it its true value.'[32] On 4 April Schumann sent a copy of the *Fantasie* to Liszt, who responded on 5 June: 'The Fantasie dedicated to me is a work of the highest order – I am truly proud of the honour you do me in addressing such a grand composition to me. Also I want to work at it and penetrate it to the core, in order to be able to draw the greatest possible effect from it.' Subsequently he told Schumann that he was prepared to play *Carnaval*, some of the *Davidsbündlertänze* and *Kinderszenen* in public, but that '*Kreisleriana* and the *Fantasie* dedicated to me are harder for the public to digest – I will reserve them until later.'[33]

While neither Clara nor Liszt was immediately prepared to introduce the *Fantasie* to the public, they were both keen to play it in private circles in which it would be better appreciated. Clara, who received her copy of the *Fantasie* while on tour in Paris, lost no time in playing it to Alkan, and she reported to Schumann on 11 June 1839 that Alkan had been delighted by it.[34] As for Liszt, he played it to Schumann in March 1840, when he visited the composer in Leipzig. Schumann mentioned the performance to Clara in a letter dated 20 March:

I wish you could have heard Liszt this morning. He really is quite extraordinary. He played from my *Novelletten*, the Fantasy, and the Sonata, in a way that affected me deeply. Much of it was different from what I had expected, but all of it was full of genius, and had a tenderness and sense of daring which is no doubt not an everyday occurrence with him.[35]

Schumann's reference to the 'tenderness' of Liszt's playing is echoed in an account left by Anton Strelezki, one of Liszt's pupils. Commenting on Strelezki's own performance of the *Fantasie*, Liszt apparently complimented him but observed that his conception of the first movement was 'totally wrong':

everyone plays this opening movement in *too vigorous* a style. It is pre-eminently dreamy, *träumerisch*, as he [Liszt] expressed it in German, and altogether the reverse of 'noisy and heavy'. I do not mean though that it should be played at all *apathetically*, for, of course, here and there are phrases which demand vigorous execution; but the whole outline of the movement should preserve more of the *dreamy* character, than it is usual to depict in it.

According to Strelezki's account, Liszt's remarks were made in 1869. As well as giving his own views on the performance of the first movement, Liszt recalled the occasion when he had first played the *Fantasie* to Schumann. After listening to the first movement Schumann had said nothing, which prompted Liszt to ask him to comment. Schumann promised to give his verdict after hearing the second movement:

I played the second movement, and with such effect that Schumann jumped out of his chair, flung his arms around me, and with tears in his eyes, cried: '*Göttlich*' ['Divine']! Our ideas are absolutely identical as regards the rendering of these movements, only you with your magic fingers have carried my ideas to a realization that I had never dreamed of!'[36]

There is a telling discrepancy between this and Schumann's own account to Clara, in which it was precisely the difference between his and Liszt's ideas which he had chosen to emphasize. And it is perhaps interesting that Schumann did not ask Liszt to play all three movements before giving his opinion. In the light of Clara's particular enthusiasm for the second movement and the strong images which it evoked in her mind, it may be that whatever 'ideas' Schumann professed to share with Liszt were in reality those kindled in him by Clara. The point of hearing the second movement, then, would have been to compare her performance with Liszt's.[37]

Despite the downturn in Clara's and Schumann's opinion of Liszt both as a performer and a person, Liszt's affection for them both and for the *Fantasie* remained strong. He apparently did include it in his public recitals during 1839–48;[38] and in a letter to Wasielewski, he admitted on 9 January 1857 that the dedication to Schumann of his own Sonata in B minor had been made in return for Schumann's dedication to him of the *Fantasie*.[39] And whatever Clara's view of his playing, Liszt continued to impart his interpretation of the *Fantasie* to his pupils, for it remained in his teaching repertoire until his very last years. Carl Lachmund reported a performance before Liszt by Emma Grosskurth on 27 May 1882. After commenting on the difficulty of the notorious coda in the second movement, Liszt sat at the keyboard and played it himself without showing any sign of strain. As Lachmund put it, 'I have heard many great pianists play the Fantasy, but all of them, even Rubinstein, displayed physical exertion in this passage. Not Liszt, however.'[40] The notes of another pupil, August Göllerich, show that the *Fantasie* was frequently studied in 1884–6, and that Liszt was wont to remark on the 'wonderful' passage repeated four times at the end of the first movement: that is, the allusive passage beginning at bar 295.[41]

Mention of piano recitals in mid-nineteenth-century journals frequently extends no further than the performer's name and the location of the event; programmes are often mentioned only vaguely. Thus it is not easy to reconstruct the early performance history of the *Fantasie* in any detail, nor even at this stage to determine anything about the first public performance. Judging by the tone of available reviews and other writings, such as the first edition of Wasielewski's biography, the *Fantasie* was well known in European concert halls by the late 1850s. A review in *SmW* of a recital given in Vienna in 1859 by Carl Debrois van Bruyck is notable not for any mention of the *Fantasie* but for its indication of Schumann's changed reception in that city: the reviewer claimed that whereas Schumann's music had formerly been largely neglected, the critical writings of van Bruyck and Hanslick had effected a major change in public opinion so that it was now rare for a Vienna concert programme not to include any music by Schumann.[42] On 29 November 1862, indeed, the Viennese public wildly applauded Brahms's performance of the *Fantasie* in the Vereinssaal, although the critic for the *Deutsche Musik-Zeitung* thought that the second movement of this 'highly poetic' (*hochpoetisch*) work had been taken too fast.[43]

That Brahms's performances of the *Fantasie* were widespread is suggested by a question put to him by Clara in a letter dated 8 December 1865: 'You didn't write and tell me how the audiences in the various venues have responded to Robert's Fantasy.'[44] It is tempting to imagine that Clara, for whom the *Fantasie* had more than usually strong autobiographical resonances, may have been anxious to let Schumann's former great protégé Brahms test public opinion of the work before finally laying her own interpretation open to scrutiny. She had told Brahms on 5 August 1859 that she had been blissfully studying the *Fantasie*;[45] but it was not until 15 December 1866 that she played it in public, at a recital in the Leipzig Gewandhaus. On this occasion the *Fantasie* shared the programme with Schubert's Quartet in A minor, Brahms's Trio in E♭, Op. 40 and Schumann's own Quartet in F, Op. 41 No. 2.[46] The *AMZ* said that it 'was played by Frau Schumann more wonderfully than we believe we have ever heard. Performed so consummately, even this work dating from Schumann's first period, when formal structure is uncertain, will achieve its full effect.' *SmW* referred to 'this ardent confession' (*glühende Bekenntnis*) from the period of Schumann's *Sturm und Drang* and noted that Clara was a particularly appropriate interpreter for the work.[47]

Again, the *AMZ* review implies that performances of the *Fantasie* were no rarity by this date. As for performances outside Europe, and outside the close circle of Schumann's intimates, *Dwight's Journal* gives some idea of the early fortunes of the *Fantasie* in America. Schumann's piano music was specially featured in a series of four recitals given in 1867 in Boston by Carlyle Petersilea, and the *Fantasie* was the opening work in the first recital on 3 January, less than a month after Clara's première in Leipzig. The review, beyond focusing on Schumann's supposed inability to handle large-scale form, suggests that individual movements of the *Fantasie* were commonly included in recitals while complete performances were less usual:

The [*Fantasie*] is equal to a large Sonata in length, and in richness and variety of matter in its three elaborate and interesting movements.

It was a well-chosen specimen, showing the individuality of Schumann, his genius (struggling with form), his depth of nature well. Hitherto we had heard only single movements of it in the concert room, and were now glad of an opportunity to hear the whole . . . It was an arduous task for the interpreter, but Mr Petersilea seemed fully master of it, and presented it in all its breadth and contrasts as a clear, consistent, vigorous whole.

The *Fantasie*, the review concluded, was 'a noble and significant work'. In view of the relationship between it and Schubert's *'Wanderer' Fantasie* explored above in Chapter 3, it is pleasing to note that Petersilea's 3 January recital ended with the Schubert work, which 'made a fine counterpart to [Schumann's]'.[48] That Schumann's *Fantasie* remained somewhat rare in American recital programmes is clear from a review of Anna Mehlig's performance at Mechanics' Hall, Boston on 17 January 1872:

The most important rarity of the concert was Schumann's great *Fantasie*, op. 17, in three long parts, through whose broad and complex web of harmonies there runs a haunting melody, half hidden in the middle part, but ever and anon rising to the surface. The first piece is mystical and dreamy, provoking a desire to understand it better; the second is march-like, bold, triumphant, not quite convincing on the first hearing; the third is in a vein of graceful, tender, sentiment which cannot appeal in vain. It is extremely difficult to play, and difficult to understand at once, however well played, as we must presume it was by one so gifted. It must be heard again.[49]

The establishment of Schumann's reputation in England seems to have been slow, certainly during his lifetime and shortly thereafter. Clara's concert tours, the first of which took place in 1856, the year of Schumann's death, played a major part in making his music better known and appreciated in London. Clara herself appears never to have played the *Fantasie* in England, however; as for native pianists, the critic Frederick Corder commented in *The Musical Times* as late as March 1889 that their most popular Schumann offerings were the first two numbers of the *Fantasiestücke*, Op. 12; 'a scrap' of the first of the *Nachtstücke*, Op. 23; the *Romanze* in F♯, Op. 28 No. 2; the first of the *Novelletten*, Op. 21; the *Arabeske*, Op. 18, and the *Schlummerlied* from *Albumblätter*, Op. 124.[50]

But the *Fantasie* was heard in London in the late nineteenth century, not least from the hands of Paderewski, who chose it for the programme of his London première at St James's Hall on 9 May 1890. *The Times* observed that 'the player's loudest tones are by no means always beautiful, but the amount of fire and passion he gave . . . to certain passages in Schumann's fantasia in C major produced a profound effect. In the [*Fantasie*] his interpretation of the passage headed 'Im Legendenton' was beyond all praise for its poetic insight. The last movement was less fully understood, but the second was magnificently played.' The frequency with which the *Fantasie* was now heard in London is suggested by the fact that in the same review the critic reported on another performance, by Franz Krummel at Steinway Hall: this was passed over merely as 'an intelligent reading'.[51]

Conclusion

Kossmaly's misgivings apart, the *Fantasie* has always been regarded as one of Schumann's most significant works. It holds a secure place in the piano repertory of the late twentieth century. But no reception history would be complete if it failed to consider Schumann's own reservations about the *Fantasie* after its publication. Writing to Hirschbach on 28 May 1839, he encouraged him to take a look at the first movement and declared that 'in its time (three years ago) I thought I had reached the heights with it – although I think otherwise now'.[52] A clue to what Schumann meant may be found in his slightly earlier letter of 15 March to Simonin de Sire, in which he gave details of his newly-published works, *Kinderszenen*, *Kreisleriana*, and the *Fantasie*, and mentioned the forthcoming *Arabeske*, *Blumenstück*, and *Humoreske*. Of all these, he declared that he liked *Kreisleriana* the best. And subsequently he claimed that his style had become consistently 'easier and smoother' (*leichter und weicher*), a significant point since the *Fantasie* was the oldest of the works mentioned.[53]

Schumann's assessment of his stylistic development here is very similar to Kossmaly's published in the *AMZ* in 1844. And the letter to Kossmaly dated 5 May 1843 bears further on Schumann's view of his earlier music. He apologized for not being able to send Kossmaly copies of the works which he considered his best: *Kreisleriana* (again), the *Fantasiestücke*, Op. 12, the *Novelletten*, and the *Drei Romanzen*, Op. 28. As for the earlier ones, which he enclosed 'with some misgivings',

you will easily discover everything immature and unfinished about them. They are mostly reflections of my turbulent earlier life; the man and musician in me were always trying to express themselves simultaneously; no doubt that remains so, although I have learned to control myself and also my art better. Your sympathetic heart will find out how many joys and sorrows lie buried together in this little pile of notes.[54]

If Schumann perceived that the *Fantasie* was stylistically backward or immature by the time it was published three years after its composition, his final comments to Kossmaly here hint at another reason for his reservations. By 1839 the *Fantasie* must have seemed 'out of date' in the sense that the emotional upheaval which had inspired certainly its first movement was now largely a thing of the past. In January 1839 Schumann had described it to Clara as 'excessively melancholy' (*übermelancholisch*), and he had used the same adjective again in April of that year when, speaking of the 'unhappy summer of 1836' which held the key to the *Fantasie*, he told Clara that 'now I have no reason to compose such unhappy and melancholy music'.[55] At this distance it is not so easy to catch the melancholic strain in the *Fantasie*. We should note Schumann's view, however, and rejoice that in the musician the sufferings of the man found so eloquent a voice.

Notes

1 The compositional history of the *Fantasie*

1 See *AMZ* 47 (1845), cols. 572–6 and 589–97. Accounts of the festivities differ in various details: see also Breidenstein, *Festgabe*; Schmoll, 'Geschichte'; Walker, *The Virtuoso Years*, pp. 417–26; and Williams, *Portrait of Liszt*, pp. 214–22.

2 *Tb* II, pp. 393–6; details of the letter to Liszt appear on p. 547, n. 699.

3 Breidenstein, *Festgabe*, pp. 1–2.

4 *NZfM* 4 (1836), pp. 121–2. This issue is dated 8 April. See *AMZ* 38 (1836), col. 247 (issue dated 13 April) for a slightly different version of the *Aufruf*.

5 For further details of the appeal, including a list of donors, see Breidenstein, *Festgabe*, pp. 4–10.

6 *NZfM* 4 (1836), p. 122, asterisked footnote to the *Aufruf*.

7 *GS* I, pp. 215–23.

8 *Tb* II, p. 25. Boetticher, *Klavierwerke*, II, p. 245 cites Schumann's letter of 14 September to Heinrich Dorn in connection with the *Fantasie*, but Schumann seems to be referring to a work by Dorn rather than one by himself: see *JNF*, no. 75, pp. 77–9.

9 Erler, *Schumann's Leben*, I, pp. 101–3. The original (*US-NYpm*) appears to give 'Obolum' for 'Obolus', a word of Greek origin meaning (in Schumann's use) a financial contribution.

10 For the letter to Haslinger see the summary quoted in *BG*, p. 262. For the letter to Breitkopf & Härtel see *JNF*, no. 486, p. 421, where Jansen supplies '[Phantasiestücke]' following 'Phantasien' in the erroneous belief that Schumann was referring to his Op. 12 collection. *JNF*, no. 81, p. 83, dated '[vom 5 Januar 1837]' mentions 'meine Sonate, die noch viel schöner werden muss', which Jansen presumes (see his n. 90) to be the 'sonata for Beethoven'. But Schumann was probably referring to his Op. 22: see Roesner, 'Schumann's Revisions', pp. 98–9, n. 8.

11 Further on Schumann's relationship to his publishers see Hofmann, *Die Erstdrucke*, especially pp. IX–X and XIII.

12 *Tb* II, pp. 41–2.

13 *Tb* II, pp. 30, 31, 32.

14 *ibid.*: 'In dieser Zeit [July–August 1837] erschienen *Carnaval* u.[nd] *Etudes symphoniques*.' That the worklist still refers to the 'Sonata for Beethoven' may indicate that it precedes Schumann's letter of 22 May to Breitkopf & Härtel, where the title 'Phantasien' first appears.

15 *Tb* II, pp. 34, 45, 44.

16 *Bw* I, p. 75; *Tb* II, p. 50; *Bw* I, p. 91. For Clara's reply see *Bw* I, p. 108.

17 *Tb* II, p. 50.

18 *JNF*, no. 488, p. 422: the '3rd piano sonata' must have been the unfinished one in F minor referred to above. The letter of 6 February is apparently unpublished; see *GB-Lbl*, Add. Ms. 33965, fol. 309: 'die *Phantasien* (die ich *Fata Morgana* nennen möchte)'.

19 *Tb* II, p. 50; *NZfM* 8 (1838), p. 52, *Anzeige von Verlagseigenthum*. Breitkopf & Härtel eventually published only the 'Phantasieen' (as the *Fantasie*, Op. 17) and the 'Novelletten' (as Op. 21).

20 *Bw* I, p. 126 (letter begun on 17 March). See also p. 121, where Schumann had described *Kinderszenen* in more detail. For details of three important misprints in the text published in *Bw* I see *Tb* II, p. 475, n. 175.

21 *Tb* II, pp. 52, 53.

22 *Bw* I, p. 145. The beginning of this huge letter (p. 133) is dated 'Sonnabend vor Ostern' – that is, Easter Saturday – by Schumann and 'Leipzig, den 13ten April 38' in Clara's hand. Schumann's diary (*Tb* II, p. 54) shows, however, that in 1838 Easter Saturday fell not on 13 but 14 April.

23 Schumann's romance with Clara Wieck began seriously in autumn 1835, and famously failed to receive her father's blessing. In February 1836 Friedrich Wieck forbade any further contact between the lovers, a ban whose length and effectiveness is sadly attested by the complete absence of any correspondence between them for the period 13 February 1836 to 13 August 1837.

24 Erler, *Schumann's Leben*, I, p. 101; Sotheby's, 23 November 1977, lot 191, and 22–3 November 1984, lot 534. The earlier Sotheby's description is palpably incorrect in various respects, not least in its description of the manuscript as being the 'first version of the score of the work later revised as the Fantasie for piano and orchestra, Op. 17'!

25 The period from March 1833 to August 1837 is covered in Schumann's diary only by a brief resumé dating from November 1838. For the year 1836 see *Tb* I, p. 422: a 'sad year' and a 'sad summer'. In June he received a letter from Clara (it has apparently not survived, but doubtless accompanied the return of Schumann's letters and requested that he return hers). On these biographical details see Litzmann, *Clara Schumann*, I, pp. 99, 109–10. For the letter to Zuccalmaglio see J*NF*, no. 71, p. 74. J*NF*, nos. 68–70, pp. 73–4, to Schumann's landlady Frau Devrient, although undated, must belong to this period also. The release which Schumann found in music brought forth not only the first movement of the *Fantasie* but also the *Concert sans orchestre*, Op. 14, which was published in September.

26 This unpublished letter is located in *D-Zsch*, Sign. 8187–A2. I am grateful to Dr Gerd Nauhaus for providing me with a transcription of the relevant passage.

27 See below, n. 49. The reference to this letter in *Tb* II, pp. 475–6, n. 177, wrongly gives the date as 20 December. Since the change of title was eventually indicated by letter, it may be that Breitkopf & Härtel never actually returned the *Stichvorlage* in accordance with Schumann's request of 6 July.

28 J*NF*, no. 493, p. 425.

29 *Bw* II, pp. 368, 418.

30 Schumann was again writing from Vienna to Breitkopf & Härtel in Leipzig and to Clara in Paris. The sentence 'Mit Diligence ist heute ebenfalls eine Correctur der Phantasie abgegangen' in the letter of 2 March (*D-DS*) is omitted from J*NF*, no. 494, pp. 425–6. The letter to Clara is *Bw* II, p. 441.

31 *Tb* II, p. 87. The letter of 20 March is unpublished (*D-DS*): 'Könnte die H[er]rn Liszt zugeignete Phantasie noch bis 4 [originally 5] April in meinen Händen sein, so würde ich sie [deleted] noch ein Exempl[ar] davon an Liszt nach Rom schicken können. Im anderen Fall ersuche ich Sie kein Exemplar nach Wien schicken zu wollen, da ich den 5ten April von *hier* abzureisen und Mitte des Monats in Leipzig einzutreffen gedenke.'

32 *Bw* II, pp. 474, 479.

33 See *Bw* II, pp. 489, 495. Clara's repeated request for the *Fantasie* and other new works, Schumann's queries as to whether she has received them, and her initially negative replies may be followed in *Bw* II, pp. 491, 507, 522, and 529.

34 *Bw* II, p. 532.

35 *NZfM* 10 (1839), p. 160. The impending publication of the *Fantasie*, and of the 2nd Sonata [Op. 22] and the *Novelletten* [Op. 21], listed as Op. 21 and 22 respectively, had been announced on 22 March (*ibid.*, p. 96).

36 *Bw* II, pp. 538, 549.

37 *Bw* II, p. 562.
38 The motto comes from Schlegel's poem cycle *Abendröte* and is discussed more fully in Chapter 3 below.
39 See further Gurlitt, 'Schumann in seinen Skizzen'; Roesner, 'Studies', especially pp. 1–142; Wendt, 'Zu Skizzenbüchern'.
40 Wendt, 'Zu Skizzenbüchern', p. 114.
41 For a photograph of the sketchleaf see Boetticher, *Klavierwerke*, I, Pl. XV. A slightly different transcription is given in Edler, *Schumann*, p. 141.
42 I have been unable to transcribe the two words written underneath bar 2 of the sketch.
43 See Boetticher, *Fantasie*, p. II, where 'frühe Einzelskizzen', amounting to 49 bars, are listed as Wiede Sign. 11/325.
44 See Leo Liepmannssohn, Versteigerungs-Katalog 60: *Autographen von Musikern*, 21–2 November 1930, lot 18. 'Obolen' may be a misreading of 'Obolum': see n. 9 above.
45 Both auction catalogues give 'Op. 16a' as the number on the title-page of the manuscript, and this reading is corroborated by Erler, *Schumann's Leben*, I, p. 101. The numbering in Plate 1 seems clearly to be just '16', however; no explanation for this slight discrepancy is presently available.
46 On the relationship between Schumann, Liszt, and the *Fantasie*, see Walker, 'A Declining Relationship'.
47 In two other places (bar 23, Pl. 1 and bars 125–6, Pl. 2) the word 'gilt' ('valid') is used to indicate that smudged or deleted passages stand.
48 It was first discussed in Walker, 'A Declining Relationship'.
49 *F-Pn*, unpublished: 'Die mit "Dichtungen" überschriebene Composition heisst besser: *Phantasie* f.[ür] Pfte. Die Dedicace lautet an Liszt. Die Opuszahl der Phantasie ist Op. 17.' Schumann's *Brief v.[on] 19/12 38* is cited as authority for the change of title in a bracketed note to the right of the word *Fantasie* in the *Stichvorlage*.
50 See Walker, 'A Declining Relationship', p. 160 for a reproduction of fol. 15v, and Boetticher's edition of the *Fantasie* referred to in n. 43 for a transcription of the original ending.
51 The reproduction of folio 2r in Walker, 'A Declining Relationship', p. 159, shows Schumann's intended device at the head of the first movement. Breitkopf & Härtel did not carry out his wishes, however.
52 Dr Robert Murányi of the National Széchényi Library kindly assisted in the transcription of these headings.
53 That these revisions were made in pencil rather than ink is of some consequence. The deletion of the three main movement headings and their replacement by the star device was done in ink. Thus it would seem that the renaming of the *Legende* belongs to a phase of revisions separate from that which suppressed *Ruinen*, *Siegesbogen* and *Sternbild*. It is even possible that the pencil emendations to Schumann's 'erzählend im Legendenton' were made not by him but by Breitkopf & Härtel. Modern editions of the work keep the *Im Legendenton* spelling.
54 *NZfM* 8 (1838), p. 65: 'Wo Mehre strebend sich verbunden' replaces the original, 'Wo mehre bildend sich in Eins verbunden': see Schlegel, *Gedichte* (1809), p. 54; (1816), p. 59. *Abendröte* occupies pp. 12–34 of the earlier and pp. 16–38 of the later edition.

2 'What's in a name?' Genre and title in the *Fantasie*

1 See Plantinga, *Schumann as Critic*, and Marston, 'Schumann's Monument'.
2 *GS* II, pp. 81–2, 177, 68.
3 *GS* II, p. 171.
4 *GS* II, p. 174. The review dates from 1837.
5 *GS* III, pp. 37–8.
6 Deutsch, *Schubert Verzeichnis*, p. 598. D. 935 was in fact intended as a continuation of the earlier set of four Impromptus, D. 899; the pieces in D. 935 were numbered 5–8 by Schubert.

7 *JNF*, no. 150, p. 150.

8 *GS* III, p. 80.

9 The fact that Schumann labelled the *Im Legendenton* section *Romanza* in the autograph score (see Chapter 1) raises further questions of genre for which there is insufficient space here.

10 See Roe, 'Autograph', and Voss, *Konzert*, pp. 163–70.

11 The relationship of the *'Wanderer' Fantasie* to Schumann's Op. 17 is pursued in Chapter 3. While the succession of movement-types in the *'Wanderer' Fantasie* is clearly derived from the sonata tradition, the succession of keys, C–c♯–A♭–C, is relatively unconventional (though less so for Schubert's own œuvre).

12 See Voss, *Sinfonie Nr. 4*, p. 140 for a facsimile of the original title-page of the autograph score of the second version (1851) bearing this title.

13 See Kahl, 'Romantic Piano Music', p. 239.

14 *GS* I, p. 204, from a review written in 1835.

15 Op. 27 No. 2, the 'Moonlight' Sonata, was surely the model for Mendelssohn's F♯ minor *Fantasie*.

16 On Schumann's understanding of Beethoven's late quartets see Marston, 'Schumann's Monument'.

17 The fact that the three movements sound and behave like independent pieces is not contradicted by the existence of a complex web of thematic interrelationships linking them at a deeper level. These interrelationships are discussed in Chapter 5.

18 *GS* III, p. 38; italics mine.

19 However, see also *Bw* II, p. 126, a letter of March 1838 to Clara in which Schumann described his (unfinished) sonata in F minor begun in 1836–7 as 'very different from the others'.

20 *GS* I, p. 308.

21 In fact Schumann's Op. 11 and Op. 22 were similarly assembled from movements written at different periods. See Roesner, 'Studies', especially Chapter 5.

22 *Bw* II, p. 473.

23 See, however, Dunsby, 'The Multi-Piece in Brahms', where the issues raised here are discussed at greater length. While his approach offers a potentially useful model for the study of Schumann's *Fantasie* collections, Dunsby emphasizes that not all 'multi-pieces' will necessarily exhibit the properties he finds in Brahms's Op. 116. Another relevant discussion is Kaminsky, 'Principles of Formal Structure'.

24 *Bw* I, p. 105 (12 February 1838): Schumann suggested that Clara might play 'Traumes Wirren' and 'Des Abends' together. 'In der Nacht', on the other hand, seemed to him to be too long. No doubt Schumann was concerned more with what the public might find acceptable at this time than with preserving the integrity of his composition. Yet even as recently as 1979–80 Vladimir Horowitz coupled the *Fantasiestücke*, Op. 111 with the third and fourth *Nachtstücke* from Op. 23; the resulting 'suite' may be experienced in the compact disc recording GD 86680.

25 See *'Fata Morgana'* in Schulz, *Fremdwörterbuch*, I, p. 208, where *Semilasso in Africa* (see below) is listed as one of the literary sources. The quotation from *Flegeljahre* in Schulz, *Fremdwörterbuch*, is taken from Book 1, Chapter 15 (*Riesenmuschel*).

26 *Tb* II, p. 49; also p. 656 for a biographical note on Pückler-Muskau.

27 *Semilasso* was first published in 1836; for an English translation see Pückler-Muskau, *Semilasso*, especially III, pp. 55 and 110.

28 *Tb* II, p. 82, and the related n. 299, p. 489.

3 Allusion and quotation in the *Fantasie*

1 The *Grossvatertanz* surfaces again in the finale to *Carnaval*, thereby strengthening the allusiveness of this work to extra-musical elements, to other music in general, and to *Papillons* in particular.

2 *Bw* II, pp. 798, 808, 812, 822. The Schumann worklist in *Grove*, XVI, p. 865, lists an

unpublished sonata movement in B♭ dating from 1836: this is presumably the composition in question.

3 For example, Solomon, 'Sonatas and Fantasie', p. 62; Daverio, '*Arabeske*', p. 160. For Schumann's 'allusion' to Beethoven see, for example, Chissell, *Schumann* (1967), p. 108.

4 Abert, *Schumann* (1910), p. 64. The first edition (pp. 58–9) contains no reference to *An die ferne Geliebte*.

5 *JNF*, p. 537, n. 507. Jansen's point was taken up in Dahms, *Schumann*, p. 287. Prior to Jansen, Reimann, *Schumanns Leben*, p. 73 had noted the imprecision of Schumann's reference to the 'Adagio' (Reimann asks 'Einleitung oder II. Satz?') of the symphony.

6 Thus, Erler, *Schumann's Leben*, I, p. 103. Abraham, *A Symposium*, p. 45, n. 2, implies that the symphony quotation was excised and does not elaborate on the 'other references to the Beethoven [song] cycle' which he hears. In the absence of Schumann's original manuscripts of the second and third movements of the *Fantasie*, the nature and extent of any revisions remains speculative. Judging by what little is known of the autograph of the first movement, however, it seems unlikely that major revisions of substance were undertaken. In this connection it may be significant that Schumann always referred to the *Fantasie* as a work of 1836: see his letter of 15 March 1839 to Simonin de Sire, or his listing of the *Fantasie* in his own *Werkverzeichnis* (photograph of the relevant page in Boetticher, *Klavierwerke*, I, Pl. 2).

7 For a modern edition of Schlegel's poems see Schlegel, *Dichtungen*, where *Abendröte* begins on p. 177.

8 *ibid.*, pp. 158–60. *Fantasie* follows closely after *Abendröte* in Schlegel, *Gedichte*. In the 1809 edition *Abendröte* ends on p. 34 and *Fantasie* begins on p. 37; in the 1816 edition the page numbers are 38 and 41 respectively.

9 Lines 1, 7, and 15.

10 Daverio, '*Arabeske*', p. 151.

11 See Deutsch, *Schubert Verzeichnis*, p. 377. The same is probably true of another of Schubert's settings of the *Abendröte* poems, *Der Fluss* (D. 693), composed in March 1820. Daverio claims that Schumann's third movement also evokes this song; but *Der Fluss* was not published until 1872 (Deutsch, *Schubert Verzeichnis*, pp. 406–7).

12 Moving beyond the passage illustrated in Example 3.3, note the even closer registral and harmonic relationship between Schubert's bars 14–17 and Schumann's third cadence on V/a in bar 12 of the *Fantasie* finale.

13 Compare the formulation in Abbate, *Unsung Voices*, p. 42, where a sequence of events in Dukas's *L'Apprenti sorcier* is compared to the opening of Saint-Saëns's *Danse macabre* in terms of 'what could plausibly be considered a musical version of intertextuality, as certain sequences refer back to specific works'.

14 D. 547, published as Op. 88 No. 4 in 1827 or 1828.

4 Form in the first movement

1 Kerman, *The Beethoven Quartets*, p. 150, referring to the slow movement of the 'Rasumovsky' Quartet in C, Op. 59 No. 3.

2 Wasielewski, *Schumann* (1858), p. 151.

3 Newcomb, ' "Between Absolute and Program Music" ', p. 240, where Newcomb is referring to the finale of the second symphony.

4 More loosely, the parallel extends to bar 105 in the first section, in that a new subsection (*Im lebhaften Tempo*) begins here while bars 103–5 are essentially repetitions of bar 102. Moreover, the succession c2–a1 in bars 292–3 might be heard as a rhythmically augmented parallel to the same succession in bars 103–4.

5 Viewed differently, bars 84–6 are the excised ones: bar 276 corresponds to bar 87, and transposition down a fifth begins at this point.

6 Wasielewski, *Schumann* (1858), pp 151–2.

7   Dahms, *Schumann*, p. 286. The *Seitenthema* is not explicitly located at bar 41, but the context ('Aus dem Sturm löst sich piano das Seitenthema, das denselben triebhaften Charakter wie das Hauptthema verrät') makes clear what Dahms has in mind.
8   Chissell, *Schumann* (1967), p. 109. In the 1948 edition (p. 117) Chissell had identified the D minor theme at bar 41 as the 'second subject'.
9   Chissell, *Piano Music*, pp. 36–7.
10   Solomon, 'Sonatas and Fantasie', pp. 65–6.
11   Daverio, '*Arabeske*', pp. 156–8.
12   *ibid.*, p. 152. In his n. 11 Daverio imputes to Chissell, *Piano Music*, p. 36 the claim that the development begins at bar 82.
13   Daverio, '*Arabeske*', p. 152, and Example 1, p. 153.
14   Newcomb, 'Narrative Strategies', p. 170.
15   Rosen, *Sonata Forms*, pp. 222, 272.
16   For Rosen, 'in all significant respects of structure and detail the Schumann Fantasy is totally unclassical': *The Classical Style*, p. 451.
17   Note that 'tonal instability' is an issue at the beginning of the development section in Daverio's reading. The development functions classically both as an extension and heightening of the dissonance set up in the exposition, and later as the preparation for the resolution. That is, the main part of the development will explore new tonal regions not yet touched upon, but will eventually work back to the dominant *chord* (as opposed to *key*) in order to prepare the return of the tonic at the beginning of the recapitulation.
18   As the Neapolitan degree relative to the prevailing tonic, D♭ is in fact not far removed from C minor; but Schumann avoids emphasizing the Neapolitan connection, strengthening thereby the sense of D♭ as a remote key area.
19   For a brief explanation of the analytical methodology and notation used in some examples in this chapter and in Chapter 5 see the Preface.
20   Daverio, '*Arabeske*', p. 161.
21   Chissell, *Piano Music*, p. 32 refers to Schumann's 'wholly unsatisfactory variation of the classical pattern, i.e. with the development section repeated after the recapitulation proper, before the coda' and notes the effect which this has of 'dissipating tension just at the moment when it most needs tautening'. For a more positive and considered approach to Schumann's formal experimentation in the piano sonatas and *Fantasie* see Roesner, ' "Parallel" Forms'.
22   See n. 3.
23   Rosen, *The Classical Style*, p. 452.
24   My reading of bars 29–34 differs significantly from that of Daverio ('*Arabeske*', p. 156 and Figure 1, p. 158), who hears this section in E♭ major and argues for a 'C/E♭ tonal juxtaposition' in the first theme group which complements the D minor/F major pairing in bars 41–81. Similarly, Roesner (' "Parallel" Forms', p. 274) understands bars 29–33 as an 'E♭-major exposition'.
25   There is of course a textural similarity with bar 29; but this appearance of the opening material is unique in not being built over a pedal harmony and should not be thought of as operating on the same 'level' as those at bars 19, 97, 119, and 286.
26   See Example 4.3 for the 'V–I' relationship between the left-hand figuration at the beginning of the movement and the chord in bar 128.
27   Furthermore, note that the syncopated and repeated-note elements in this theme derive from bars 14–15, the tail of the initial thematic statement.
28   As for the actual deceptive resolution in bars 156–7 which introduces the melodic reference to bars 295–7, this is identical (transposition apart) to that in bars 96–7 of Section 1: compare Example 4.7.
29   Recall the suggestion in Example 4.6c that bar 225 also realizes the resolution sidestepped or 'displaced' following bar 118.
30   This reference to the tonality of bars 41–81 and 225–73 in terms of a main key incorporating

a subordinate one pursues the earlier analysis summarized in Figure 4.1. This reading may be compared with Daverio's 'tonal pairings' D minor/F major and C minor/E♭ major in 'Arabeske', p. 158.

31 In contrast to bar 96, bar 285 resolves exactly as expected: compare Example 4.5a above.

5 Schlegel's *leiser Ton* and thematic unity in the *Fantasie*

1 Wasielewski, *Schumann* (1880), p. 117. This criticism was prompted by Schumann's own slightly disparaging remarks about the first movement in a letter to Herrmann Hirschbach dated 28 May 1839 (not 9 June 1839, as stated in Wasielewski, *ibid.*): see Chapter 7 for further details.

2 All further references to Example 5.2 are given in the form of the group number followed by the bar number in which the particular element begins. Thus the two elements already discussed are I, 2 and II, 295.

3 That the formal organization of the second movement constantly thwarts our expectations is explained in the next chapter. At issue here is the extent to which there is little doubt as to what constitutes a theme in this movement.

4 It may be significant that the only apparently independent thematic element in Example 5.7 is the left-hand one beginning in bar 30 (and repeated at bar 87) which Jansen took to be Schumann's homage to the Allegretto of Beethoven's Seventh Symphony: see Chapter 3 above.

5 The bracketed b[1] in the first bar of the top stave of Example 5.8 derives from the accompaniment at this point. The rhythm of the passage creates the effect of a melodic line c^2–b^1–c^2, an exact transposition of the 'parent' line in bar 41.

6 *GS* II, pp. 51–2. The review appeared originally in *NZfM* 5 (1836), p. 68.

7 *Bw* II, p. 367. The Schumann worklist in *Grove*, XVI, p. 866 claims that *Guirlande* is identical with the *Blumenstück*, Op. 19, a claim found elsewhere which ought not to be accepted uncritically. (Similarly, on p. 865 *Phantasien* is given as the original title for the *Fantasiestücke*, Op. 12, whereas it actually belongs to the *Fantasie*, Op. 17 – see page 23.)

6 Form in the second and third movements

1 Wasielewski, *Schumann* (1858), p. 152; (1906), p. 170; Dahms, *Schumann*, p. 287; Chissell, *Schumann* (1967), p. 109; Roesner, ' "Parallel" Forms', p. 276.

2 Moreover, the strategy of transposing down a tone and repeating an extended segment from the first part of the movement while nevertheless omitting the opening of the movement itself is one that Schumann had also employed in the first movement, beginning at bar 225.

3 The beginning of subsection *a2* (bars 40–53) in March I, like the whole of the initial section *A*, is not repeated at all.

4 Dahms, *Schumann*, p. 287; Solomon, 'Sonatas and Fantasie', p. 67; Chissell, *Schumann* (1967), p. 109; Wasielewski, *Schumann* (1858), p. 152; (1906), p. 170; Dale, 'Piano Music', p. 47; Roesner, ' "Parallel" Forms', pp. 276–7.

5 For Roesner, *ibid.*, p. 276, 'the finale [like the first movement] is based on the poetic idea of a hard-won attainment of a tonal goal', and that tonal goal is reached at bar 119, where 'the true tonic . . . triumphs' (p. 277 and Figure 7). My interpretation differs significantly on both points.

6 Again, compare the first movement, where in bars 61–81 an apparently stable F major is deflected to D minor.

7 *JNF*, no. 140, pp. 136–7.

7 The subsequent history of the *Fantasie*

1 *JNF*, no. 115, pp. 109–10. For de Sire's letter to Schumann see *BG*, no. 126, pp. 179–81.

2 The article on Schumann in Schilling, *Encyclopädie*, VI, pp. 281–4, is a notably early and favourable assessment of his music, obviously predating the composition of the *Fantasie*.

3 *JNF*, no. 150, p. 150.

4 *Bw* II, pp. 577–8.

5 *BG*, no. 25/II, p. 48.

6 *JNF*, no. 250, p. 227.

7 Kossmaly, 'Schumann's Claviercompositionen'.

8 For Kossmaly's article see *Dwight's Journal of Music* 9 (1856), pp. 173–5, 181–2. The quotations are taken from pp. 174 and 182. See also vol. 34 (1875), pp. 363–4 for a later article, by Ernst Pauer, discussing Schumann's style and briefly mentioning the *Fantasie*.

9 Ker, 'Traum'. On Köhler see Vogler, *"Signale"*, p. 132.

10 Wasielewski, *Schumann* (1858), p. 151.

11 Abert, *Schumann* (1910), p. 64. I am grateful to Julian Rushton for suggesting that Abert was probably thinking of the passage beginning at bar 9 in the overture to *Euryanthe*, a passage which derives from Adolar's music at 'Ich bau' auf Gott und meine Euryanth'' in Act 1 No. 4. In addition to various rhythmic, harmonic, and textural similarities, the passages from *Euryanthe* share the key of Eb with the second movement of the *Fantasie*.

12 Abert, *Schumann* (1903), p. 58.

13 See, for example, Wörner, *Schumann*, p. 122, and the English literature discussed below.

14 Abert, *Schumann* (1903), p. 58.

15 Dahms, *Schumann*, p. 286.

16 Hausegger, 'Beziehungen zwischen Tonausdruck und Bild', p. 438.

17 Menotti, 'Robert Schumanns "Grosse Sonate"', p. 146.

18 Schauffler, *Florestan*, p. 297. See also Chissell, *Schumann* (1989), pp. 80–1, where the Nocturne from Clara's *Soirées musicales*, Op. 6 is cited in this connection.

19 See the articles by Sams listed in the Bibliography; also Fiske, 'A Schumann Mystery'.

20 Roesner, ' "Parallel" Forms' represents one attempt to counter this view.

21 Dannreuther, *The Romantic Period*, pp. 241–2, 245. It should not go unremarked that Niggli, *Schumann* and Patterson, *Schumann* ignore the *Fantasie*, though Blom's revision of Patterson repairs the omission with a brief editorial reference on p. 33.

22 Dale, 'Piano Music', p. 46.

23 Chissell, *Piano Music*, pp. 36, 38.

24 Solomon, 'Sonatas and Fantasie', pp. 41, 44.

25 Rosen, *The Classical Style*, pp. 451, 453.

26 Gruber, 'Fantasie', especially pp. 123, 125–6. Gruber's article is not cited by Daverio, although both authors draw upon the same primary and secondary sources – notably, in the latter case, the work of Karl Konrad Polheim.

27 Daverio, '*Arabeske*'; Newcomb, 'Narrative Strategies'. For critiques of Newcomb see Nattiez, 'Narrativity in Music?' and Abbate, *Unsung Voices*, especially pp. 24–6, 49–52; Roesner, ' "Parallel" Forms', pp. 265, 266.

28 See Hofmann, *Die Erstdrucke*, pp. XXXVIII, 47.

29 See Reich, *Clara Schumann*, pp. 252–7. For Brahms's correspondence with Clara concerning the edition of the *Fantasie* see Roesner, 'Brahms's Editions', pp. 279–81.

30 See Musikantiquariat Hans Schneider, Katalog Nr. 188: *Robert Schumann* (Tutzing 1974), lot 156. The arrangement, made by August Horn, was advertised in the *AMZ*, 2. Jahrgang, dated 4 September 1867.

31 See, for example, Clara's letters of 5 and 26 November and Schumann's comments of 1 December, to which Clara responded two days later (*Bw* II, pp. 776, 802–3; 809–11; 812).

32 For details of Schumann's correspondence with Liszt see *BG*, p. 283. Liszt's letter to Schumann is *ibid.*, p. 111.

33 See Liszt, *Correspondance*, pp. 105–6.

34 *Bw* II, p. 566.

35 Quoted from Burger, *Liszt*, p. 129. It is likely that Liszt also played the *Fantasie* to de Sire: see the commentary to the latter's letter of 26 January 1838 in *BG*, p. 316.

36 Strelezki, *Chats with Liszt*, pp. 4–5.

37 There can be no doubt that Clara played the *Fantasie* for Schumann: in October 1840, for example, he noted (*Tb* II, p. 107) 'Studiren hörte ich [Clara] . . . Phantasie u.[nd] Kreisleriana von mir.'

38 An entry by Clara in *Tb* II, p. 197 referring to Liszt's Leipzig concert on 16 December 1841 has occasionally been misunderstood to suggest that Liszt performed the *Fantasie* in public and 'in dreadful taste' on this occasion: see for example Reich, *Clara Schumann*, p. 214. The work in question was actually Liszt's own Fantasy on Themes from *Robert le Diable* (Clara writes '*Robert*-Fantasie'): for the programme of the recital see *NZfM* 16 (1842), p. 23. I have been unable to trace a review of any recital in which Liszt performed the *Fantasie*. However, the 'Programme général des morceaux exécutés par F. Liszt à ses concerts de 1838 à 1848', compiled by A. Conradi and revised by Liszt and transcribed in Walker, *The Virtuoso Years*, pp. 445–8 contradicts Walker's earlier assertion in 'A Declining Relationship', p. 164, that Liszt 'never played the Fantasie in public at all'.

39 Liszt, *Briefe*, I, p. 256. Contrary to Walker, 'A Declining Relationship', p. 164, nothing in this letter suggests that Liszt harboured any regrets about not having played the *Fantasie* in public.

40 Williams, *Portrait of Liszt*, p. 600. Niecks, *Schumann*, p. 184, mentions a performance of the *Fantasie* by Rubinstein in the fourth concert of his 1885–6 season.

41 Jerger, *Liszts Klavierunterricht*, pp. 48–9, 95, 96, 141. See also Ramann, *Lisztiana*, p. 408: Liszt reaffirmed his high opinion of the *Fantasie* in March 1880.

42 *SmW* 17 (1859), p. 577. An article on Schumann by Louis Ehlert, *ibid.*, pp. 425–9, mentions the *Fantasie* as one of the main products of Schumann's first period, 'die exaltirte Zeit Jean Paul'scher und Hoffmann'scher Anregungen'. See *JNF*, no. 406, pp. 355–6 for a letter from Schumann to van Bruyck (10 May 1852) in which the latter's critical activities on Schumann's behalf are mentioned.

43 Reviews in *SmW* 20 (1862), p. 689 and *Deutsche Musik-Zeitung* 3 (1862), p. 389. A review in *SmW* 13 (1855), p. 389 shows that in his Bremen recital on 20 November 1855 Brahms played Beethoven's *Fantasie*, Op. 77 and not Schumann's Op. 17, as claimed by Litzmann, *Schumann, Brahms: Briefe*, I, p. 149.

44 Litzmann, *Schumann, Brahms: Briefe*, I, p. 520.

45 *ibid.*, p. 270.

46 Neither this nor any other performance of the *Fantasie* is listed in Dörffel, *Geschichte*. Pianists who gave works by Schumann during the period covered by Dörffel include (excepting those mentioned here in the main text) Hans von Bülow, Carl Tausig, Emma Brandes, and Agnes Zimmerman.

47 *AMZ*, 1. Jahrgang (1866), p. 419; *SmW* 25 (1867), p. 8, where the date of the recital is erroneously given as 15 November.

48 *Dwight's Journal* 26 (1867), p. 382.

49 *ibid.* 31 (1872), p. 175.

50 Information in this paragraph is taken from Scholes, *The Mirror of Music*, pp. 420–2, 314, 307.

51 *The Times*, 13 May 1890, p. 4.

52 *JNF*, no. 159, p. 156.

53 *JNF*, no. 150, pp. 148–51.

54 *JNF*, no. 250, p. 227.

55 *Bw* II, pp. 368, 495.

Bibliography

Abbate, Carolyn. *Unsung Voices: Opera and Musical Narrative in the Nineteenth Century* (Princeton, New Jersey 1991)

Abert, Hermann. *Robert Schumann* (Berlin 1903); 2nd edn. (Berlin 1910)

Allgemeine musikalische Zeitung (Leipzig 1798–1848; 1863–5; 1866–82)

Boetticher, Wolfgang. *Robert Schumanns Klavierwerke: neue biographische und textkritische Untersuchungen.* I: Op. 1–6 (Wilhelmshaven 1976); II: Op. 7–13 (Wilhelmshaven 1984)

(ed.) *Briefe und Gedichte aus dem Album Robert und Clara Schumanns* (Leipzig 1979); 2nd edn. (Leipzig 1981)

(ed.) *Robert Schumann: Fantasie Opus 17* (Munich [1987])

Breidenstein, Heinrich Carl. *Festgabe zu der am 12ten August 1845 stattfindenden Inauguration des Beethoven-Monuments* (Bonn 1845; repr. Bonn 1983)

Burger, Ernst. *Franz Liszt*, trans. Stewart Spencer (Princeton 1989)

Chissell, Joan. *Schumann* (London 1948); 3rd edn. (London 1967); 5th edn. (London 1989)

Schumann Piano Music (London 1972)

Dahms, Walter. *Schumann* (Berlin and Leipzig 1916)

Dale, Kathleen. 'The Piano Music', in *Schumann: A Symposium*, ed. Gerald Abraham (London 1952), pp. 12–97

Dannreuther, Edward. *The Oxford History of Music Vol. 6: The Romantic Period* (Oxford 1905)

Daverio, John. 'Schumann's "Im Legendenton" and Friedrich Schlegel's *Arabeske*', *Nineteenth Century Music* 11 (1987), pp. 150–63

Deutsch, Otto Erich. *Franz Schubert: Thematisches Verzeichnis seiner Werke in chronologischer Folge*, ed. Walther Dürr and others (Kassel 1978)

Deutsche Musik-Zeitung (Vienna 1860–2)

Dörffel, Alfred. *Geschichte der Gewandhausconcerte zu Leipzig vom 25. November 1781 bis 25. November 1881* (Leipzig 1884)

Dunsby, Jonathan. 'The Multi-Piece in Brahms: *Fantasien* Op. 116', in *Brahms: Biographical, Documentary and Analytical Studies*, ed. Robert Pascall (Cambridge 1983), pp. 167–89

Dwight's Journal of Music, a Paper of Art and Literature (Boston 1852–81)

Edler, Arnfried. *Robert Schumann und seine Zeit* (Laaber, 1982)

Erler, Hermann. *Robert Schumann's Leben. Aus seinen Briefen geschildert.* 2 vols. (Berlin 1887)

Fiske, Roger. 'A Schumann Mystery', *The Musical Times* 105 (1964), pp. 574–8

Gruber, Gernot. 'Robert Schumann: Fantasie op. 17, 1. Satz: Versuch einer Interpretation', *Musicologica Austriaca* 4 (1984), pp. 101–30

Gurlitt, Willibald. 'Robert Schumann in seinen Skizzen gegenüber Beethoven', in *Kongressbericht der Beethoven-Zentenarfeier* (Vienna 1927), pp. 91–4

Hausegger, Friedrich von. 'Beziehungen zwischen Tonausdruck und Bild, erläutert an der Phantasie op. 17 von Schumann', in *Gedenken eines Schauenden: gesammelte Aufsätze*, ed. Siegmund von Hausegger (Munich 1903), pp. 425–40

Hofmann, Kurt. *Die Erstdrucke der Werke von Robert Schumann* (Tutzing 1979)

Jerger, Wilhelm. *Franz Liszts Klavierunterricht von 1884–1886 dargestellt an den Tagebuchaufzeichnungen von August Göllerich* (Regensburg 1975)

Kahl, Willi. 'Romantic Piano Music 1830–1850', in *Romanticism (1830–1890)*, ed. Gerald Abraham. New Oxford History of Music Vol. 9 (Oxford 1990)

Kaminsky, Peter. 'Principles of Formal Structure in Schumann's Early Piano Cycles', *Music Theory Spectrum* 11 (1989), pp. 207–25

Ker [Christian Louis Heinrich Köhler]. 'Traum. Wahrheit und Dichtung', *SmW* 17 (1849), pp. 321–3

Kerman, Joseph. *The Beethoven Quartets* (London 1967)

Kossmaly, Carl. 'Ueber Robert Schumann's Claviercompositionen', *AMZ* 46 (1844), cols. 1–5, 17–21, 33–7

Liszt, Franz. *Franz Liszt's Briefe*, ed. La Mara. 8 vols. (Leipzig 1893–1902)
Franz Liszt: Correspondance, ed. Pierre-Antoine Huré and Claude Knepper ([Paris] 1987)

Litzmann, Berthold. *Clara Schumann: ein Künstlerleben, nach Tagebüchern und Briefen.* 3 vols. (Leipzig 1902–8); 6th–8th edn. (Leipzig 1923–5; repr. Hildesheim and New York 1971)

(ed.) *Clara Schumann, Johannes Brahms: Briefe aus den Jahren 1853–1896.* 2 vols. (Leipzig 1927; repr. Hildesheim and New York 1989)

Marston, Nicholas. 'Schumann's Monument to Beethoven', *Nineteenth Century Music* 14 (1991), pp. 247–64

Menotti, Giovanni. 'Robert Schumanns "Grosse Sonate für das Pianoforte" für Beethovens Denkmal', in *Die Geheimdokumente der Davidsbündler* (Leipzig 1934), pp. 133–54

Nattiez, Jean-Jacques. 'Can One Speak of Narrativity in Music?', *Journal of the Royal Musical Association* 115 (1990), pp. 240–57

Neue Zeitschrift für Musik (Leipzig 1834–)

Newcomb, Anthony. 'Once More "Between Absolute and Program Music":
Schumann's Second Symphony', *Nineteenth Century Music* 7 (1984), pp. 233–
50

'Schumann and Late Eighteenth-Century Narrative Strategies', *Nineteenth
Century Music* 11 (1987), pp. 164–74

Niecks, Frederick. *Robert Schumann*, ed. Christina Niecks (London 1925)

Niggli, Arnold. *Robert Schumann. Sein Leben und seine Werke* (Basel 1879)

Patterson, Annie W. *Schumann* (London 1903); 2nd edn. rev. and ed. Eric Blom
(London 1934)

Plantinga, Leon B. *Schumann as Critic* (New Haven and London 1967)

Pückler-Muskau, Hermann Ludwig Heinrich, Furst von. *Semilasso in Africa:
Adventures in Algiers and Other Parts of Africa*. 3 vols. (London 1837)

Ramann, Lina. *Lisztiana: Erinnerungen an Franz Liszt in Tagebuchblättern, Briefen
und Dokumenten aus den Jahren 1873–1886/87*, ed. Arthur Seidl, rev. Friedrich
Schnapp (Mainz [1983])

Reich, Nancy B. *Clara Schumann: The Artist and the Woman* (London 1985)

Reimann, Heinrich. *Robert Schumanns Leben und Werke* (Leipzig 1887)

Roe, Stephen. 'The Autograph Manuscript of Schumann's Piano Concerto', *The
Musical Times* 131 (1990), pp. 77–9

Roesner, Linda Correll. 'Studies in Schumann Manuscripts: With Particular
Reference to Sources Transmitting Instrumental Works in the Large Forms'
(unpublished dissertation, University of New York 1973)

'Schumann's Revisions in the First Movement of the Piano Sonata in G Minor,
Op. 22', *Nineteenth Century Music* 1 (1977), pp. 97–109

'Brahms's Editions of Schumann', in *Brahms Studies: Analytical and Historical
Perspectives*, ed. George S. Bozarth (Oxford 1990), pp. 251–82

'Schumann's "Parallel" Forms', *Nineteenth Century Music* 14 (1991), pp. 265–
78

Rosen, Charles. *The Classical Style: Haydn, Mozart, Beethoven* (London 1971);
rev. edn. (London 1976)

Sonata Forms (New York and London 1980)

Sadie, Stanley, ed. *The New Grove Dictionary of Music and Musicians*. 20 vols.
(London 1980)

Sams, Eric. 'Did Schumann Use Ciphers?', *The Musical Times* 106 (1965), pp.
584–91

'The Schumann Ciphers', *The Musical Times* 107 (1966), pp. 392–400

'The Schumann Ciphers: A Coda', *The Musical Times* 107 (1966), pp. 1050–1

Schauffler, Robert Haven. *Florestan: The Life and Work of Robert Schumann* (New
York 1945)

Schilling, Gustav, ed. *Encyclopädie der gesammten musikalischen Wissenschaften,
oder Universal-Lexicon der Tonkunst*. 7 vols. (Stuttgart 1835–42; repr. Hildesheim
and New York 1974)

Schlegel, Friedrich. *Friedrich Schlegels Gedichte* (Berlin 1809); neueste Auflage (Vienna 1816)

Dichtungen, ed. Hans Eichner (Munich, Paderborn, Vienna, and Zurich 1962). Kritische Friedrich-Schlegel-Ausgabe, ed. Ernst Behler, Vol. 5

Schmoll, J. Adolf gen. Eisenwerth. 'Zur Geschichte des Beethoven-Denkmals', in *Festschrift zum 70. Geburtstag von Joseph Müller-Blattau*, ed. Christoph-Hellmut Mahling (Kassel 1966), pp. 246–51

Scholes, Percy A. *The Mirror of Music 1844–1944*. 2 vols. (London and Oxford 1947)

Schulz, Hans. *Deutsches Fremdwörterbuch*. 7 vols. (Strasburg, Berlin and New York 1913–83)

Schumann, Robert. *Gesammelte Schriften über Musik und Musiker*. 4 vols. (Leipzig 1854); repr. with epilogue by Gerd Nauhaus. 2 vols. (Wiesbaden 1985)

Robert Schumanns Briefe: neue Folge, ed. F. Gustav Jansen (Leipzig 1886); 2nd edn. (Leipzig 1904)

Tagebücher. I: 1828–1838, ed. Georg Eismann (Leipzig 1971); II: 1836–1854, ed. Gerd Nauhaus (Leipzig 1987)

and Schumann, Clara. *Briefwechsel: kritische Gesamtausgabe*, ed. Eva Weissweiler. I (Basel and Frankfurt am Main 1984); II (Basel and Frankfurt am Main 1987)

Signale für die musikalische Welt (Leipzig 1843–1941)

Solomon, Yonty. 'Solo Piano Music I: The Sonatas and Fantasie', in *Robert Schumann: The Man and His Music*, ed. Alan Walker (London 1972), pp. 41–67

Strelezki, Anton. *Personal Recollections of Chats with Liszt* (London 1887)

Vogler, Rudolf. *Die Musikzeitschrift "Signale für die musikalische Welt" 1843–1900* (Regensburg 1975)

Voss, Egon, ed. *Robert Schumann: Konzert für Klavier und Orchester a-Moll, op. 54* (Mainz 1979)

(ed.) *Robert Schumann: Sinfonie Nr. 4, d-Moll, op. 120* (Mainz 1980)

Walker, Alan. 'Schumann, Liszt and the C Major Fantasie, Op. 17: A Declining Relationship', *Music and Letters* 60 (1979), pp. 156–65

Franz Liszt: The Virtuoso Years 1811–1847 (London 1983)

Wasielewski, Joseph Wilhelm von. *Robert Schumann: eine Biographie* (Dresden 1858); 3rd edn. (Bonn 1880); 4th edn., ed. Dr Waldemar von Wasielewski (Leipzig 1906)

Wendt, Matthias. 'Zu Robert Schumanns Skizzenbüchern', in *Schumanns Werke – Text und Interpretation*, ed. Akio Mayeda and Klaus Wolfgang Niemöller (Mainz 1987), pp. 101–19

Williams, Adrian. *Portrait of Liszt by Himself and His Contemporaries* (Oxford 1990)

Wörner, Karl H. *Robert Schumann* (Zurich 1949; repr. Munich 1987)

Index